Horizon

SPRING, 1964 · VOLUME VI, NUMBER 2

Salon des Refusés

In putting together a magazine, no matter how hard you try, there is always something left over. What gets omitted doubtless reveals something about the editors, and it is in this self-revelatory spirit that we take you behind the scenes in the planning of this issue.

It was fairly easy for us to turn down an article entitled "Will There Be a New Cultural Explosion if Harold Stassen is Elected?" It was somewhat harder to reject some designs for an improved currency. The most inventive idea was a new bill in the amount of $1.89, the so-called "Gimbel's Two," for women shoppers. And then there was a proposal for a World's Fair Exhibit depicting this country as it will be, if present trends continue, in the year 2611—that is, with one person for every square foot of space in the entire U.S.A. Unfortunately, the authorities at the Fair do not seem to have adopted this type of Futurama.

It was almost impossible for us to say no to Hans Oppenheimer, a poet of Ajijic, Jalisco, Mexico, who writes American Haiku, according to the spirit if not the letter of the classic Japanese verse form. (They have seventeen syllables, like Hirohito's prize winner just before Pearl Harbor: *Peaceful is morning in the shrine garden; world conditions, it is hoped, also will be peaceful.* Something like that.)

Here is one of Oppenheimer's Haiku:

> *Man comes and goes*
> *But while he's here*
> *He fills the wastebaskets*
> *Higher and HIGHER and HIGHER.*
> *It ain't right.*

And another:

> *Put on my pack*
> *And hiked down Wall Street;*
> *Saw a banker cry tears.*
> *Hied me to Madison Avenue*
> *Saw an Ad-man cry tears.*
> *Why*
> *Do they cry*
> *With the spring in the air*
> *And the churches so close?*

Well, just one more:

> *They said it couldn't be done!*
> *So nobody did it.*
> *And everybody said:*
> *"You see—I told you so!"*
> *Except one little man*
> *Living on the other side of the world*
> *In a cave*
> *Under a big pile of rocks.*
> *HE hadn't heard that it couldn't be done,*
> *So he tried.*
> *He couldn't do it, either.*

Resolution is a weak thing, and we only wish we had had space for an urgent proposal from one of our editors. There are, he asserts, some simple but necessary inventions which might better our world. He listed them this way. CELLAR: A large hole in the ground, directly under the house, replacing the usual crawl space. Ideal for storing furniture, sleds,

PUBLISHER: James Parton   EDITORIAL DIRECTOR: Joseph J. Thorndike, Jr.

EDITOR: Marshall B. Davidson

ASSOCIATE EDITOR: Ralph Backlund   ASSISTANT EDITORS: Jane Wilson, Shirley Abbott, Charles L. Mee, Jr., Mary Cable, Barbara Klaw   EDITORIAL ASSISTANTS: Wendy Buehr, Priscilla Flood   LIBRARIAN: Caroline Backlund   COPY EDITOR: Mary Ann Pfeiffer   *Assistant:* Joan Rehe

SENIOR ART DIRECTOR: Irwin Glusker   ART DIRECTOR: Elton Robinson

ADVISORY BOARD: Gilbert Highet, *Chairman,* Frederick Burkhardt, Richard M. Ketchum, Oliver Jensen, Jotham Johnson, John Walker

EUROPEAN CONSULTING EDITOR: J. H. Plumb, *Christ's College, Cambridge*
EUROPEAN BUREAU: Gertrudis Feliu, *Chief, 11 rue du Bouloi, Paris Ier*

ᴄHORIZON

A Magazine of the Arts

SPRING, 1964 · VOLUME VI, NUMBER 2

boxes, spare lumber, tools, etc. Frees garage for its primeval purpose of housing automobile. (A related convenience is an ATTIC, formed by covering house with a V-shaped roof instead of a flat one.) ALL-PURPOSE DOCTOR: Replaces surgeon, internist, gynecologist, dermatologist, pediatrician, psychoanalyst. Solves problem of what to do when you ache all over and don't know which specialist to call. Suggested name: general practitioner.

 AIRLINE PARACHUTE: This is simply a civilian version of the familiar military parachute used to such good purpose by aviators. Passenger slips it on before entering plane. When crash seems imminent, passenger jumps out of plane, thus saving life. DINING ROOM: This replaces the customary television room. Provides stable chairs and table for meals. Enables children to take eyes off TV set and see what they are eating. Enables parents to get good look at children and find out how they live. SMALL WINDOW: Ideal for living rooms. No more need to stare at neighbor's laundry all day. No glare from hot sun. No cringing in night clothes from sight of passers-by. Makes family feel at home instead of on street. TROLLEY CAR: Attractive vehicle that replaces bus. Runs by electricity on tracks which can be laid along curbs, thus for first time actually enforcing "No parking" rules on major streets. Roomy, sturdy, free of oil and gasoline fumes, thus lowering incidence of lung cancer in cities.

Well, we wish there had been room for all this.

THE EDITORS

HORIZON is published every three months by American Heritage Publishing Co., Inc. Executive and editorial offices: 551 Fifth Ave., New York, N.Y. 10017. HORIZON welcomes contributions but can assume no responsibility for unsolicited material.

All correspondence about subscriptions should be addressed to: HORIZON Subscription Office, 379 West Center St., Marion, Ohio 43301.

Single Copies: $5.00
Annual Subscriptions: $16.00 in the U.S. & Can.
$17.00 elsewhere

Annual indexes for Volumes I–IV priced at $1 have been published every September. The index for Volume V will be published in April, 1964, as will a cumulative index for Volumes I–V priced at $3. HORIZON is also indexed in the *Readers Guide to Periodical Literature.*

Title registered U.S. Patent Office
Second-class postage paid at New York, N.Y., and at additional mailing offices.

COVER: One of the apparently irresistible themes in art is the legend of Judith, the beautiful Jewish widow who seduced Nebuchadnezzar's general, Holofernes, in order to cut off his head. This regal profile is a detail from Andrea Mantegna's pen-and-brush treatment of the subject, which successfully emphasizes the heroic rather than the bloodcurdling aspects of the story. The drawing, dated 1491, is in the Uffizi Gallery in Florence. It is reproduced in full in an article on Mantegna beginning on page 70.

*A sketch of the main gallery
at the Barnes Foundation, Merion, Pa.
This corner is hung with Cézannes and Renoirs,
but the room also contains Matisses,
Picassos, a Tintoretto, a Daumier, and a Glackens.*

ILLUSTRATED FOR HORIZON BY DAVID LEVINE

FOR THE RABBLE"

Thus did the late Albert C. Barnes describe the gallery housing his superb art collection. An effort to get the taxpaying rabble past its tax-exempt gates was made by our author—with what success, you will see

By LOIS G. FORER

There are more than forty thousand foundations in America today, dedicated to many thousands of causes, including providing lollipops for children, Christmas dinners for horses, and pin money for presidents' wives. The laws governing them are surprisingly vague. Has the public a legal right to benefit from a foundation, since it is tax-exempt? Can a man use his private property as he wishes? Is foundation property private property? Are the trustees and directors of a foundation accountable to the state for their stewardship of funds? These and many other moral and legal questions were raised, but not fully explored, in the case of the Commonwealth of Pennsylvania vs. The Barnes Foundation, a case which I, as Deputy Attorney General of Pennsylvania,* brought into court.

The Barnes Foundation, of Merion, Pennsylvania, founded in 1922 by Dr. Albert C. Barnes, owns, among many other art works, the finest collection of French post-impressionist painting in the United States; elsewhere, its only rivals were the Shchukin and Morosov collections in Moscow and Leningrad, now held by the state. For many years neither the Barnes nor the Russian collections could be seen by the public at large. Interestingly enough, both the Soviet government and the Barnes Foundation deny this indisputable fact.

Since its inception the Barnes Foundation has been the despair and exasperation of art lovers throughout the world who have been rudely barred from its doors. Art books carry plaintive notes explaining that certain significant paintings are "believed" to be in the possession of the Barnes Foundation but may not be seen or reproduced.

The feud that Dr. Barnes carried on with the art world is amply documented by his grossly insulting notes written to many distinguished people. For example, Barnes wrote to Sir

---

* The author is not now employed by the Commonwealth of Pennsylvania. The views expressed here are hers alone and not necessarily the official policy of Pennsylvania.

Kenneth Clark, one of the world's leading art critics and the former director of London's National Gallery, as follows:

Jan. 23, 1951

Dear Clark:

Your recent letter telling me of your proposed visit here prompts me to inform you that all participants in the current ballyhoos of the institution which has been widely publicized as "The House of Prostitution of Art and Education on the Parkway," are barred from admission to the Foundation's gallery.

Very truly,
Albert C. Barnes

Barnes was here referring to the Philadelphia Museum of Art, whose directors had earned his permanent hatred in the early twenties by criticizing his collection. Newspaper files of the period reveal that the very journals and art critics who have since acclaimed the Barnes collection did indeed greet it in the twenties with savage denunciations and ridicule. The pictures were characterized as "degenerate," "unclean," or "the work of insane persons." Barnes's pique at the Establishment in the art world is understandable. But his critics mellowed with time and learned to understand and appreciate Modigliani and Matisse, if not their sponsor, while Barnes maintained his fierce hostility until death. The feud has been continued by the trustees of the Foundation, who have resolutely barred members of the art-world Establishment.

But the favored few who have managed to be admitted to the gallery are staggered by the dazzling, overwhelming magnitude of the collection: more than thirty-five Renoirs are on display (nobody knows the exact number of anything, as there is no published catalogue); many Cézannes; several roomfuls of Matisses; a number of Picasso's finest paintings of the Blue and Rose periods; and a superb canvas by Seurat, for which the Louvre was once rumored to have offered $500,000—to say nothing of paintings by Titian, Goya, El Greco, and many other masters, African sculpture, Chinese art, American artifacts, and miscellaneous other treasures. The collection has been evaluated at from one to two hundred million dollars. In addition the Foundation has liquid assets of ten million dollars, and two valuable properties. But in more than forty years of existence, it has never had to account to any agency of the state government for its stewardship of all this wealth.

In 1951, shortly after the death of Barnes, the *Philadelphia Inquirer* unsuccessfully sued to compel the opening of the gallery to the public. The Supreme Court of Pennsylvania, in dismissing this taxpayer's suit, declared that only the state government has standing to question the conduct of a foundation. When I became Deputy Attorney General of Pennsylvania and was assigned to the supervision and regulation of charities, I determined that the state should test the right of an art gallery to be exempt from state taxes and still exclude the public. In 1958, on behalf of the Commonwealth of Pennsylvania, I filed an action against the Foundation and its trustees to show cause why the public should not be admitted to the Barnes art gallery. Thus began a strange and bitter adventure. Now that the litigation is over, I am at liberty to set forth the facts and delineate for the consideration of the thoughtful public the important issues still unresolved.

When I brought suit against the Foundation, the public interest which I was representing was an abstraction. Of course, I knew that there were many people who wanted to see the collection, many people who hated Barnes and scoffed at the Foundation, and some people who considered that the Foundation was very well administered. But it never occurred to me that a lawsuit involving an art gallery would be front-page news in the metropolitan papers day after day. I did not anticipate that citizens who were neither artists nor art historians would become embroiled, that public meetings would be held and money raised to "defend" the multimillion-dollar Foundation, or that its partisans would picket visitors to the gallery and write scurrilous letters to the Governor. But then, I did not know the Barnes Foundation.

The anecdotes about Barnes himself are numerous, varied, and in some cases unprintable. Apparently he was a man of strong opinions who evoked equally strong responses, and this, perhaps, is why I found it very difficult to obtain reliable information about him. He was born in Philadelphia in 1872. He was a poor boy, but managed to attend the University of Pennsylvania medical school, from which he was graduated. He went to Germany for several years. He returned to Philadelphia and shortly thereafter began the manufacture of Argyrol, an antiseptic used in the treatment of infections of the eyes and mucous membranes, and made at least five million dollars. Some say that he invented the formula; others that it was really invented by his partner, who subsequently disappears from all accounts of Barnes's life. Some say that he was a financial wizard; others that he was just lucky. For whatever reason, it is a fact that he sold the Argyrol business before the advent of antibiotics. Some say that he was a

profoundly intellectual man of deep understanding; others that he merely picked the brains of his friends and associates. Both John Dewey and Bertrand Russell came to the Foundation and lectured there. Dewey had the highest praise for him; but Russell and Barnes disagreed, and Russell was obliged to sue Barnes for his salary.

Even the purchase of the paintings is clouded with controversy. Did Barnes himself select the paintings? Or did he rely entirely upon his artist friends—on William Glackens, for instance, whom he once sent to Paris with twenty thousand dollars and instructions to buy French impressionists? Mrs. Barnes described to me an occasion on which Barnes saw a painting in a window of an obscure gallery in Paris. He was taken with the picture, made inquiries about the artist, immediately went in a taxi to the unknown artist's atelier, and promptly purchased, for a very small price, a great number of this artist's paintings. Thus, according to Mrs. Barnes, was Soutine discovered. But Barnes's detractors maintain that when he relied upon his own judgment, he made mistakes. Professor S. J. Freedberg, of the Department of Fine Arts at Harvard, and Professor Frederick Hartt, Chairman of the Art Department of the University of Pennsylvania, have asserted that more than two dozen of the collection's "Renaissance" paintings are, in fact, twentieth-century forgeries.

In starting the state's proceedings against the Barnes Foundation, I was confronted with almost thirty years of exceedingly disagreeable behavior on the part of Dr. Barnes; but since the law wisely limits testimony regarding the dead on the proper theory that a man should be entitled to confront his accusers and speak for himself, I restricted the complaint against the Foundation to the years subsequent to Barnes's death. Despite his eccentricities and vulgarity and his obsessional opinion that only he and his followers could understand "plastic values," the fact remains that he did amass one of the most extraordinary single collections of painting in his time, that he housed it in a magnificent gallery and endowed his Foundation with ample funds to maintain it in perpetuity. For this, I believe, we should all be grateful. The same considerations do not apply to the trustees; they neither earned the money nor collected the paintings. Their duties and responsibilities are defined not only by the laws of Pennsylvania, but also by the deed of trust establishing the Foundation in 1922. This is a very long document with numerous amendments, all carefully drawn by the late Owen J. Roberts, who later became a justice of the United States Supreme Court. Despite its legal precision, the irascible vitality of Barnes animates the document. He states clearly what his intentions are: "It will be incumbent upon the Board of Trustees to make such rules and regulations as will ensure that the plain people, that is, men and women who gain their livelihood by daily toil in shops, factories, schools, stores, and similar places, shall have *free* access to the art gallery and the arboretum upon those days when the gallery and arboretum *are to be open to the public* . . ." (Italics mine.)

In 1931, when Barnes testified in a case testing the tax-exempt status of a certain Foundation property, he revealed more about himself than he did about the Foundation. He declared: "It [the art gallery] is no place for the rabble. I have nothing to say against the rabble, only that it is a rabble. I came from the rabble, as I think most of our people did—what was once the rabble. The only thing is, we have risen." Unfortunately this supercilious contempt for the common man, rather than concern for his education and welfare, seems to have motivated Barnes's successors.

The essence of the Complaint was that the trustees are duty bound to give free admission to the plain people under the indenture. It took two years, innumerable arguments, pleadings, and briefs, and a decision of the highest state court to get the Foundation *even to file an answer*. In effect, the defendants maintained that the Foundation was under no obligation to answer to the state, that the Foundation was an educational institution and as such did not have to admit the public, and besides that the public was admitted and always had been admitted to the art gallery. The Barnes defendants have persisted in this kind of now-you-see-it-now-you-don't type of argument until this very day.

The pretentious educational claims of the Foundation are open to question. For years the proud boast that she had been admitted to the Barnes Foundation course was a prized status symbol of a certain type of intellectually ambitious middle-class matron of the Philadelphia area. In the earnestness and fanaticism of this small group of Barnes graduates, most of whom are women, one finds almost the qualities of a cult. The common characteristics of its members seem to be personal intensity and serious, humorless devotion to "culture." The Barnes collection is sufficiently modern to appeal to those eager to be in the intellectual know, and yet not so contemporary as to require a risk of judgment in acclaiming an unknown who may not meet the test of time.

I learned that the course is a two-year sequence for which no tuition is charged. The first-year lectures are given by a Miss Violette de Mazia, a mysterious figure of whom we learned some surprising things in the course of the trial. She is a small, thin woman of uncertain age, generally wearing sandals, a dirndl, beads, and dark glasses, with her hair in a shoulder-length bob—and is the high priestess of the Foundation. Her sole stated function appears to be the delivery of one three-hour lecture a week, from October to June. For this she receives ten thousand dollars per annum.

Attendance is the *sine qua non* of these lectures. Two unexcused absences and the student is expelled in disgrace. Many a successful business or professional man has had to put off his vacation plans lest his wife be cast into outer darkness for missing one of Miss De Mazia's lectures. But mere physical presence is the only requirement: there are no recitations, no examinations, no papers. Yet attendance is not so easy as it sounds. Ask any college student if he can listen intelligently to three uninterrupted hours of lecturing! Physical as well as mental endurance is essential, for there are no coffee breaks and no recesses, not even for imperative calls of nature.

Approximately seventy people are admitted to this course each year. No one has been able to ascertain the criteria for admission. Each applicant is personally interviewed by Miss De Mazia, and some are promptly rejected. The reasons for rejection are never given, but apparently it is safer not to mention any previous background in art or aesthetics. Others are invited to the initial lecture and are then told to reapply the next year. *Mene, mene, tekel, upharsin.* In checking over the list of students for the year 1961–62, I discovered that more than three-fourths were housewives. The remainder were principally retired men or professional men, and there were also a few college students. The poor working people so solicitously specified by Barnes as the beneficiaries of the Foundation were nowhere to be found among the students. I presume they were busy toiling in the shops and factories, as most people are on a weekday afternoon.

Of the seventy or so who are lucky enough to be chosen each year, several may be expected to drop out. Those who survive the first year are eligible for a second year of similar lectures. Since Dr. Barnes's death, there has been no artist or educator of professional renown associated with the Foundation. During Barnes's life many distinguished people came to the Foundation. Young artists received scholarships, and many have gone on to careers as artists or professors.

In discussing the content of the present lectures with former students, I found it extremely difficult to obtain any coherent account of the course. And there is no syllabus. The University of Pennsylvania and other educational institutions in the area refuse to recognize the Barnes courses for credit on the grounds that the teachers are unqualified. Some of the people who have taken the course say that it is the most moving and inspiring educational experience of their lives. These devotees include intelligent college graduates as well as mere enthusiasts. But the severest critics of the Foundation are also to be found among the former students.

Jon D. Longaker, Chairman of the Division of the Arts of Randolph Macon College, wrote to me after receiving a plea from the "Friends of the Barnes Foundation" for funds to fight the state, and volunteered the following opinion:

That the "educational work" of the Foundation is of extremely poor caliber any unbiased educator would agree. I saw it in operation both as a student and as a teacher there. There were only two classes being taught in 1946–7, amounting to a maximum total of six hours a week! I felt then and still feel that this "educational work," while it is no doubt a sincere (though misguided) thing, has always been used as an excuse for excluding the public from the gallery.

The philosophy and educational principles of the Foundation are expounded in *The Art in Painting* by Barnes, published in 1926. Embedded in a great deal of long-winded prose is a quite ordinary message: appreciation of art requires study; a painting is to be looked at for its design, its "plastic qualities," its color and form, rather than for any subject matter or mere prettiness, and so on. In short, the mystery-

TEXT CONTINUED ON PAGE 90

FOUR FACES
OF HERESY

One is puritan, one messianic, one mystical, and one
rational. All torment the established church until
they become part of the Establishment themselves

By H. R. TREVOR-ROPER

A heretic recants in this detail from The Conversion of an Arian by Saint Remy, *painted c. 1500 by the so-called Master of St. Gilles*

An account of religious heresy, in a single essay! What an undertaking! Only once in history, to my knowledge, has so vast a subject been comprehended in one work, and that was in the *Impartial History of the Church and the Heretics*, published by the Lutheran pietist Gottfried Arnold in 1699. The example is not entirely propitious. Arnold's two volumes, which consisted of twenty-three hundred double-column folio pages—and there were fewer heresies then than now—raised a storm that lasted a generation. He was denounced by his contemporaries as an infamous falsifier of history; the most judicious of Lutheran historians described him as an ignorant, impertinent disturber of the peace of the Church; and one critic declared that he had written "the most wicked book since the birth of Christ." From this it will be easily deduced that Arnold, on the whole, took the side of the heretics.

But Goethe (and who would not wish to be on the same side as Goethe?) thought differently. When Arnold's book fell into his hands, he was enchanted by it. It had, he wrote, a great influence on him. Now he saw the heretics of history in a new light. "I had often heard it said," he wrote, "that every man came in the end to have his own religion, and now it seemed to me the most natural thing in the world that I should devise my own; which I did with great comfort. . . ."

To devise one's own religion—that is, in fact, exactly what heresy is. It is the literal meaning of the word. Heresy is private choice, the opposite of orthodoxy which is not chosen but imposed and accepted. For this reason there is a great difference between heresy and schism, for schism does not necessarily imply choice, or if it does, it is not private choice. A schismatic church is a church that has broken away, en bloc, as the Eastern Church broke away from the Western in the Middle Ages and the Protestant Church from the Catholic at the time of the Reformation. Schism may begin in heresy, just as orthodoxy may (Christianity began as a Jewish heresy), but it need not. The Roman Catholic Church regards the Anglican Church as schismatic, not heretical. And a schismatic church soon builds up its own orthodoxy and begins to persecute its own heretics. The pure heretics are those who never created an established church or an orthodoxy and whose members came to it by personal choice.

Even so, what hundreds of them there are! Every generation in the two thousand years of the Christian church has produced them, and their recondite doctrines have never ceased to enrage the orthodox and amuse the infidel. Turn up any century at random: it is like turning up a stone in a well-kept formal garden. Above, all is smooth and quiet, but underneath there is a scurrying of disturbed wood lice and trotting centipedes that cause the orthodox nose to wrinkle in disgust but delight everyone who enjoys the rich variety of Nature. In the third century we will find the Ebionites, the Basilidians, the Valentinians, the Marcionites. In the fourth, the Donatists, with their extremists the Circumcellions, divided Africa from Europe, while the Arians divided East against West. In the fifth, the Nestorians, the Eutychians, the

The great English heretic John Wycliffe suffered the posthumous indignity of having his bones dug up, burned, and cast into the river

Apollinarians, and the Monophysites convulsed the Byzantine Empire with their metaphysical speculations. There is no end to the list. If we are to make an end, we must select, or we must find some principle of continuity, reducing the multitudinous species to a few intelligible families.

This is not easy, for the history of heresy is subject to a general obscurity. Most of it has been written by outraged champions of orthodoxy, more eager to condemn than to understand. The works of the heretics themselves have been destroyed. Nevertheless, if we keep our heads, we may be able to restore the distinctions which indignation has blurred and see the continuity which has been hidden under a multiplicity of names.

For in fact, when we look closely at these heresies, we soon find that for every dozen names there is only one idea. The great heresies are not the fanciful notions of underemployed monks, each trying to be more original, or more absurd, than the other; they are recurrent ideas which break through the continually sealed crust of orthodoxy because they contain an important truth or an irrepressible human aspiration. They are not confined to one religion. Pre-Christian ideas cropped up as Christian heresies, pre-Islamic ideas as Islamic heresies, and some Christian and Islamic heresies have been interchangeable. Some heresies have been absorbed into orthodoxy, at least for a time; very few have been permanently excluded from it.

Let me give a few instances of the process. Consider Arianism, the doctrine that the Father is a good deal more important than the Son, let alone the Holy Ghost. This doctrine was declared heretical at the Council of Nicaea in 325, and after half a century of ding-dong struggle (for some of the emperors were Arians), it was stamped out of the more sophisticated provinces by the first of the Spanish Inquisitors, the emperor Theodosius the Great. But it survived for a time in remote frontier provinces and was embraced by the Goths and Vandals who carried it to Spain and Africa; and, though bruised, it survived even longer in the East. There, in the fifth century, it took a new shape as Nestorianism. Suppressed by the Byzantine emperors, it did not entirely perish: with the Moslem conquests it merely took on a new, Moslem color. Whatever the pundits might say, the doctrine that God is one, not three, continued to seem more plausible to simple-minded barbarians, and if they were not allowed to believe it of Jehovah, they would change his name and believe it of Allah. Later the idea crept back into the Christian church and was held, in even more extreme form, by some less simple-minded barbarians of remote provinces: by Servetus, who discovered the mechanism of the heart, and was burned alive by Calvin amid universal applause; by Joseph Priestley, who identified oxygen, and whose house was burned down around him by the orthodox citizens of Birmingham; and by Sir Isaac Newton, who rearranged the universe, and, after dying in his bed at the age of eighty-five, was carried to his tomb in Westminster Abbey by competing earls and dukes

and the Lord High Chancellor of England. (But this transformation came about because of an important new fact, to which we will turn our attention later.)

Or again, consider the two doctrines that competed with Christianity for the soul of the young Saint Augustine—Manichaeism and Neo-Platonism. Manichaeism was a Persian heresy maintaining that the world was governed by the interplay of two independent positive forces, the spirits of good and evil. Neo-Platonism was a late Greek mixture of mysticism and mathematics, in which the Platonic doctrines of the divinity that pervades the universe and the human soul were preserved by allegorizing all that was inconvenient in them. When Christianity prevailed, these defeated rivals did not perish: they became movements within it and enjoyed a long Christian history. Manichaeism was ruthlessly put down in the Eastern Empire in the sixth century by that great lawgiver, builder, and persecutor, the Louis XIV of Byzantium, the emperor Justinian. It then reappeared in Armenia as the Paulician heresy, and after it was crushed there, turned up in the Balkans where it flourished, especially in Bulgaria, under the name of the Bogomil heresy. Extirpated once again in the eleventh century, it moved still farther west, and cropped up in southern France as the Albigensian heresy, the heresy of the Cathars (the pure). This was perhaps the most hated of all heresies until the Reformation; it was the heresy par excellence, the first to be legally punished by death. By crusade and Inquisition, it was exterminated, but it has left some traces in modern languages. The word "Cathar" became the German word for heretic (*Ketzer*), while the word "Bulgar" was adapted in other languages to denote a less speculative form of nonconformity.

The history of Neo-Platonism is much less sanguinary, partly because the ideas of Neo-Platonism were much more abstract: they were embraced by conservative philosophers, not radical prophets. Consequently, once Christianized it was never officially declared a heresy. Still, some incautious Neo-Platonists, especially after the Reformation, found themselves heretics, and some, like the philosophers Giordano Bruno and Giulio Cesare Vanini, were even burned as such. As a Christian movement Neo-Platonism cropped up in fourteenth-century Germany, in fifteenth-century Florence, in seventeenth-century Germany and England. It had a great influence on the development of science from the last days of antiquity to the eighteenth century, and also on the romantic movement in literature. Goethe wrote that Neo-Platonism lay at the basis of his own private religion; it was the religion also of William Blake.

Once we recognize that the heresy of twenty centuries, though as infinite as private choice, is not random but keeps to certain well-defined channels, it becomes possible to see past the multitudinous polysyllabic names to a few constant forms. If we do this, we may be able to go further: we may discover that these swarming individualists were not merely, as the orthodox have always maintained, the miscellaneous maggots which it has been necessary from time to time to

THE METROPOLITAN MUSEUM OF ART, ROGERS FUND 1915

stamp or steam out of the majestic fabric of the Church, but also, as Gottfried Arnold supposed, people with continuous traditions of their own to which we may owe a debt.

Almost all the recurrent heresies of the Christian church have fallen, basically, into four main categories. They have been puritan and evangelical; or they have been millenarian and messianic; or mystical and quietist; or rational and critical. These four categories are not by any means mutually exclusive: the great periods of religious ferment have always seen a merging of types and thus the pullulation of intermediate heresies. But they are, it seems to me, the four main sources from which, or from whose intermixture, all particular heresies are derived, and so I will say something of all of them. All of them look back, in different ways, to the teaching of Jesus and the primitive Church. All of them oppose, or at least ignore, the far more elaborate church structure built up in the days when the Church had triumphed in the Roman Empire and become a great department of state. All of them were considered "heretical" because of this fact: because they presumed to "choose" between the real, solid, bureaucratic, political church of their own time, and the simple, imaginary church of the "unforgettable age of the apostles." When it came to a showdown, the real church, with its fire and fagot, was real; the imaginary church was imaginary.

Let us take the puritans first. Undoubtedly the early Church was puritanical. So were its Old Testament models. The prophets, from Elijah to John the Baptist, had been puritans, denouncing the gay polytheism, the local cults, the jolly beanfeasts of the Syrian tribes that surrounded and seduced the grim people of God. All through the first three centuries after Christ, the Church had kept itself pure from similar contamination. The early Christian writers had denounced such unedifying pagan habits as the burning of incense, the "impious and detestable" practice of sprinkling holy water, the absurd use of candles and votive pictures, the "profane, damnable, impious" cult of images, etc., etc. Such practices, the Christians thought, were exactly the kind of things which the prophets had denounced and which Christ had ordered them to ignore, saying that mercy was better than sacrifice, evangelical poverty and mutual charity better than sophisticated profusion or pharisaical ritual. So the early Christians kept themselves apart from society, trying to live like the first disciples, without compromise, in "apostolic poverty" and "primitive communism," a self-contained, puritan "out-group" in the secular, pagan world.

Unfortunately the virtues of a sect can rarely be preserved in an established church, and when Constantine made Christianity the official religion of the Empire, the bishops soon yielded to the temptations, or the necessities, of power. Little by little the Christian clergy took over some of the methods of the pagan priests whom they had replaced. With the pagan temples they adopted the pagan sacrifices. Pagan gods became Christian saints. "Apostolic poverty" was forgotten. And the puritan virtues were left, as the unvalued relics of

The first heretic was Simon Magus, mentioned in Acts. Later writers accused him of being able to fly. Benozzo Gozzoli's painting not only shows him aloft, supported by demons, but also grounded—fatally—at the behest of Saint Peter (left).

an outworn chrysalis stage, to the heretics who refused to move with the times.

The first "puritan" heretics were the Donatists of the fourth century. They were strong in rural North Africa—always (even when it became Islamic in religion) a puritan area. They believed that corrupt, or time-serving, priests—the priests, in fact, who had complied with the persecuting edicts of Diocletian—invalidated the sacraments which they administered, a moral view no established church can afford to hold. In eighth-century Byzantium there was another puritan revolt—this time headed by puritan emperors—against the "images," the costly pagan magnificence of the Church. And this "iconoclastic" movement has recurred often since. We think especially of Reformation Europe and Cromwellian England, when preachers, distinguishing between "the living images of God," mankind for whom Christ died, and the "dead images" of the Church to which they had been sacrificed, led mutinous crowds to topple the statues, slash the pictures, hew down the organs, and shatter the stained-glass windows of the Gothic churches.

With puritanism—the hatred of hierarchy and wealth—went evangelical poverty and community of property; sometimes also refusal of military service or of infant baptism. The established church always distrusted these subversive ideas, but in every century little communities of heretics clung to them. The monasteries—at least in their beginnings—were "communist" bodies within the Church, and the friars—again in their beginnings—were exponents of apostolic poverty. But monasteries and friars soon became rich and corrupt; their original doctrines were condemned; and the communities which clung to them were denounced as heretics. Nevertheless, such communities have continued to appear, from the Waldenses of the twelfth century to the Shakers and other utopian communist sects of nineteenth-century America. The fifteenth-century Bohemian Brethren, the seventeenth-century Quakers, and other sects refused military service, just as the early Christians had done under the pagan empire. Infant baptism was rejected by numerous sects, of which the sixteenth-century Anabaptists were by no means the first. Such rejection emphasized that church membership was not hereditary or automatic but a rational "choice"—a heresy.

Puritanism, evangelical communism, came direct from the Bible. So did the second heretical tendency, messianism. The first disciples of Christ held several extravagant notions popular among the persecuted Jews of his time. In particular, they believed—Christ himself had said it—that the end of the physical world would come in their own time; and they looked forward to the Last Judgment, the thousand-year reign of the saints, and the violent destruction of the profane world. These doctrines, a mixture of Old Testament and Christian prophecies, were brought into sharper focus after the death of Christ, by the great Jewish revolt and the destruction of the Temple of Jerusalem by Vespasian. Their most famous expression was in the book of the Apocalypse, in which the pagan Roman Empire was clearly designated as the earthly Babylon, ripe for destruction.

But, once again, the fourth century brought a change. When Rome became a Christian state, and the Christian church began to enjoy secular power, the orthodox gradually lost the taste for revolutionary doctrines. If the secular state were to blow up, the established church would blow up, too, and that did not now seem so desirable. So the old texts were reinterpreted. The Apocalypse was omitted from the canon of Scripture by the Council of Laodicea; Saint Augustine afterward explained it away as a pious allegory; and in 431 the whole idea of the millennium was condemned at the Council of Ephesus as a superstitious aberration. Those who insisted on clinging to the pre-establishment ideas of Christianity found themselves heretics; and convincing themselves (as heretics do) that they were the only true Christians, they still looked on Rome, though now Christian, as Babylon and on its ruler as the betrayer of Christ, Antichrist.

When Biblical interpretation could lead to such practical inconveniences as this, clearly something had to be done about the Bible. One answer which, as we have seen, was found useful, was to evade inconvenient or unedifying texts by representing them as allegorical. Unfortunately allegory is a game at which two can play, and before long the established church would find that while its tame theologians were using it to explain away subversive texts, impertinent heretics were using it to explain away useful and orthodox texts. In the end the Church would come to the view that the best thing to do with the Bible was to suppress it altogether: to keep it firmly locked up in dead languages and to dole out to the people only such texts, and such interpretations, as

could not possibly raise any doubts about the divine basis of the established church and all its practices.

The heretics who dodged the inconvenient texts of Scripture by allegory and symbolism relied ultimately on mysticism. Not all mystics, of course, were heretics: it depended on which texts they dodged. But the basic theory of mysticism was always heretical, for it implied that direct personal inspiration could undermine the literal meaning of the Bible. This not only gave a dangerous latitude of interpretation, which might be misused; it also implied that the individual could have access to God without availing himself of the costly apparatus of the Church. Naturally the Church looked askance on such ideas. In order to retain control of Biblical interpretation, it built up the concept of "tradition"—i.e., the collected, mutually consistent body of its own reinterpretations—to which, in the end, it gave equal authority with the Bible, and in which, though always with some hesitation, it incorporated the visions of the more conservative mystics. To the less conservative mystics it showed no mercy. Alumbrados were burned in Catholic Spain, Pietists persecuted in Lutheran Germany. As a consequence, these sects became more radical. At certain times extremists appeared who claimed that their direct relations with God exempted them from all common beliefs and justified them in the most outrageous actions. Such were the egomaniac messiahs who captured control of radical religious movements in the Middle Ages and in the sixteenth and seventeenth centuries. Such also were the adepts of "the Free Spirit," who believed that "to the pure all things are pure" and scandalized the orthodox by behaving accordingly: Bohemian Adamites, French Libertines, German Anabaptists, and English Ranters.

However dangerous, an injection of mysticism was necessary to the Church. Periodically it reinflated the sagging body. It also lifted it over some of the jagged texts of Scripture which might otherwise have punctured it. But not everyone is capable of skipping lightly over solid difficulties, and there have always been some men, even within the Church, who insist on facing them, even if they are thereby forced to disturbing consequences. At first such men were few. Critics could stay outside the Church, and converts, when they swallow, swallow whole. But with the rise of learning in a Christian society, Biblical critics arose who were not afraid of following their rational conclusions even into heresy. They were never very many, but their impact was great. It was they, for instance, who, in the sixteenth century, refloated the long-wrecked hulk of Arianism and converted the simple, puritan intolerance of barbarian tyrants into the rationalized belief of a Servetus or a Priestley. It was they who, slowly

The most celebrated early heretic was Arius, a sad-eyed Alexandrian cleric who held that God was one, not three. He was anathematized in 325 by the Council of Nicaea, at whose feet he lies in this sixteenth-century fresco in Heraklion, Crete.

and painfully, built up the irreversible science of Biblical criticism, and thereby devalued orthodoxy and heresy alike.

Puritanism, millenarianism, mysticism, rationalism—these, then, are the four permanent sources of heresy. None of them are necessarily heretical; all of them, at times, have been contained within the Church. Nor need they be radical. All have been held, at times, by fundamentally conservative men. But at certain times, and in certain places, something has happened to swell these streams into a flood, threatening the whole structure of the Church and society. One of these floods occurred in the twelfth and thirteenth centuries in Western Europe; another during the Reformation and the religious wars of the sixteenth and seventeenth centuries. By studying these periods we may come to some conclusions about the significance of heresy and its contribution to society.

The remarkable thing about the twelfth- and thirteenth-century outburst of heresy was its universality. In the Byzantine Empire there had been some spectacular heresies. Government had been convulsed, archbishops had hurled anathemas at each other, and armies of barbarous monks had been thrown into action to decide between the single or the dual nature of Christ. But these recondite heresies, more often than not, had been slogans in the long struggle for power between the churches of Constantinople and Alexandria. The really important heresies—the permanent heresies which had their roots in the Bible and in society and would recur again and again—had risen sporadically: the Donatists in fourth-century Africa, the Paulicians in seventh-century Armenia, iconoclasm in eighth-century Constantinople. But now a whole crop of such heresies occurred at one time, and all over Christendom. In Lyons a rich merchant, Peter Waldo, gathered a congregation of Waldenses, or Poor Men of Lyons, and preached a crusade to restore the Law of Christ. In Lombardy a puritan sect, the Umiliati, similarly preached and practiced the evangelical virtues; in Umbria Francis of Assisi created the cult of Holy Poverty; in France, Germany, and Italy Arnold of Brescia, a pupil of the learned Abelard, denounced the temporal power of the pope; and in Paris, in 1209, a prophet was burned for declaring the pope to be Antichrist. Meanwhile, in southern France the most ascetic, most highly organized of all heretics, the Albigenses, openly challenged the Church by setting up a rival organization. They had their own clergy, the *perfecti*, and their own laity, the *credentes*; they had their own theology, based on Manichaean dualism, which refused any compromise with the forces of evil, and among the forces of evil they numbered, especially, the established church of Rome.

Finally, at the same time there was a recrudescence of those millenarian doctrines which the Church thought it had allegorized out of existence. In the toe of Italy a studious abbot, Joachim of Floris, extracted from the Scriptures "scientific" prophecies which proved that the last great age of the world was about to begin (it would begin, said his more exact commentators, in 1260). Then all institutions, including the church of Rome, would wither away, and the kingdom of saints, without clergy or sacraments, would be established on earth, to endure till the Last Judgment. As if to illustrate these theories, a crop of messiahs also appeared. Two were Tanchelm of Antwerp, who began by denouncing clerical vices and exactions and ended by claiming the properties of Christ and distributing his bath water as a sacramental beverage to his followers, and Eon de l'Estoile, who declared himself King of Kings and partner of God and swept through the woods of Brittany destroying churches and monasteries in order to maintain his "court" of rapacious peasants. Such lunatic messiahs would crop up in every great period of heresy. The most famous was "John of Leiden," who in 1534 put himself at the head of the Anabaptist revolution in Münster and inaugurated scenes of license that were to curdle the blood of the Establishment for generations.

Naturally such an epidemic of heresy alarmed the papacy. At first the popes tried to contain the movement. They cultivated Joachim of Floris and tried to make use of his prophecies. Though they hanged Arnold of Brescia and then burned his body, they sought to win over the Umiliati and the Waldenses. With the Umiliati they succeeded, but the Waldenses would not be controlled: they retired to the mountains of Bohemia, to merge with later heretics, and to the Alps, where they were periodically massacred by orthodox peasants. The most famous massacre, in 1655, inspired Milton's sonnet:

Avenge O Lord thy slaughter'd saints, whose bones
Lie scatter'd on the Alpine mountains cold,
Ev'n them who kept thy truth so pure of old
When all our fathers worship't Stocks and Stones.

But Rome's most signal triumph was the winning over of the Franciscan movement. Although there was always a "spiritual" party among the Franciscans, which resisted the worldly embrace of the Establishment, the order itself was tamed: the early biographies of Saint Francis, which emphasized his dangerous doctrines, were burned, and ultimately, in 1322, the doctrine of apostolic poverty was itself condemned as heretical. By that time the Franciscans were rich and powerful, firmly on the side of orthodoxy and even reaction.

These were important victories; but it had been a near thing. The greatest danger had been in the early thirteenth century, when all these heresies, which formed a subversive International throughout Europe, nearly found a territorial base. For the toughest of all the heretical movements, the Albigensian Church, was patronized by a rich and independent dynasty, the counts of Toulouse. It was to scotch this danger that the greatest of medieval popes, Innocent III—who had already launched the Fourth Crusade, which brought the "schismatic" Church of Constantinople back into the fold, and parcelled the ruins of the Byzantine Empire among greedy Frankish and Italian princes—now proclaimed another and bloodier crusade against the heretical Cathars and parcelled the rich but ruined lands of Languedoc among the predatory noblemen of northern France. Thereafter the new order of Saint Dominic was fashioned into a shock corps of orthodoxy and the Roman Inquisition was established to prevent heresy from ever reaching such proportions again.

For three centuries these measures were successful. Admittedly heresy was not extinguished: the very remedies devised against it, by increasing the abuses of the Church, intensified the protest against them. In 1260—the year in which, according to Abbot Joachim, the rule of the saints was to begin —troops of messianic puritans appeared in Italy and scourged themselves throughout the towns, calling on all to repent. From Italy the movement spread to other countries. Unable to control it, the Church condemned it in 1349. Later in the fourteenth century Wycliffe led a puritan "Lollard" revolt, and popular preachers in England and elsewhere advocated a return to primitive equality. In the fifteenth century Wycliffe's ideas created revolution in Bohemia, which nearly became the territorial basis of a new international revolution. But in the end all these protests were effectively silenced; the Bohemian radicals, the Taborites, were crushed as the Albigenses had been; Wycliffe's revolt, in Milton's words, was "but a short blaze, soon damped and stifled"; and the radical heresies frequently ended in mystical resignation. For mysticism, whether heretical or not, is often the refuge of defeated radicalism. The messianic Taborites of Bohemia, after their defeat, became pacifist, mystical Bohemian Brethren just as, afterward, in defeat, the messianic German Anabaptists would become pacifist, mystical Mennonites, and the messianic English "Fifth-Monarchy Men" would become pacifist, mystical Quakers. The fourteenth and fifteenth centuries, the years when heresy was crushed and yet the Church was not reformed, were the great centuries of European mysticism: the Neo-Platonic mysticism of the Germans Suso and Tauler, the Dutch mysticism of Ruysbroeck and Thomas a Kempis, the English mysticism of Margery Kempe and Richard Rolle.

Then came the great new outburst of heresy in the sixteenth century. Against the background of the previous centuries, there is little that is new in the Reformation. Only this time international heresy obtained a secure territorial basis and prevailed. At least, some forms of it prevailed; and by prevailing became orthodoxies, established churches themselves. But others did not. Anabaptism, Socinianism, and a dozen other varieties of "permanent" heresy struggled along, outside the reach of Rome, in the interstices of protestant societies. Sometimes they made a bid for power, as the Anabaptists did in Münster in 1534 and again in England in 1653. Because of their numerical weakness, such heretics always needed the support of messianic doctrines and so fell under the control of fanatics and were destroyed. More often they contracted out of the established society and cultivated evangelical virtues in private corners, hoping that one day their time would come.

Has their day ever come? In a sense, I think that it has. For the modern world owes far more to these heretics than it is aware of. Exactly how much it owes is uncertain, and not everyone would agree with my argument; but I believe that modern society, this extraordinary society which, from its basis in Europe, has transformed the whole world, was created in large part by the heretics. They did not create it intentionally—no doubt they would be horrified if they saw it— but nevertheless it was largely their work. Certainly it was not the work of orthodoxy.

Consider the orthodox world. From the days of Constantine, Christian orthodoxy attached itself to the Roman world, a world of solid, hierarchical, bureaucratic power; and from that world it acquired its own character: the character which the heretics regarded as a betrayal of the real inheritance of Christ. In the Dark Ages the solidity of the Church served society well, but by the twelfth century, in a period of great economic growth, the tensions appeared; and they appeared, especially, in the areas of economic activity: in Lombardy, in the Rhineland, in Flanders, in Bohemia, and in the rich commercial cities of Languedoc. Moreover, it is notable that the "primitive christian" communities were generally communities of textile workers or miners. The Albigenses were also known as *Textores* (weavers). The Flemish heretics were mostly weavers. The Umiliati worked in the textile industry of Milan. The Waldenses were recruited in Lyon by a cloth merchant. The Taborites were mostly Bohemian miners, and the other centers of Central European heresy were Saxony and Silesia, the mining areas of Germany. Now cloth-working and mining were the only two great industries of the Middle Ages. Altogether the heretic International of the twelfth century can be seen, in part, as a general rejection of the institutions of feudal society by the laity, and the solid cells of resistance were to be found in the small, scattered units of European industry. Moreover, when the established church triumphed, what happened? It doubled and redoubled its own feudal bureaucratic structure, absorbed more and more of Europe's wealth and talent, and became a heavy burden on Europe's economy. The years from 1300 to 1450 in Europe, the years of the medieval counter-reformation, are generally admitted to be a period of economic decline, in which the great promise of the earlier centuries came to nothing.

The same thing can be said of the sixteenth-century Reformation. The heretics of the Reformation came largely from the economically advanced areas. Many of their leaders came from the merchant classes; the most stubborn of their martyrs were Anabaptists in the clothing towns of England, Flanders, and the Rhineland, and in the mining towns of Germany. When the established church triumphed over the Reformation, it was once again by doubling its "bureaucratic" structure. Just as the Catholic Church of the thirteenth century triumphed over heresy by the creation of new orders (the friars) and the Roman Inquisition, so in the sixteenth century it triumphed by the creation of new orders (the Jesuits) and the Spanish Inquisition. And the result was the same. Just as the years from 1300 to 1450 were years of economic stagnation in Europe, after the promise of the twelfth century, so the years 1600 to 1750 were years of economic stagnation, after the promise of the Renaissance, in those countries of Europe from which heresy was driven out.

For the Counter Reformation of the sixteenth century, unlike that of the thirteenth century, was not complete. Over a large part of Europe—Protestant Europe—it failed; and in those Protestant countries where it failed, economic expansion was continued. It was continued not so much by the orthodox, even there, as by the heretics, and particularly by the heretics squeezed out from the Catholic countries. It was Calvinists and Mennonites driven from Flanders who founded the industries of the Ruhr. It was Baptists and Quakers who made the industrial revolution in England. It was the Pietists of Saxony who began the industrialization of East Germany. And the greatest industrial power of today, America, lived in its formative period on the heretics of all Europe.

But our debt to heresy does not stop there. The advance of science also owes more to heresy than to orthodoxy. For at every stage, orthodoxy has tended to restrain intellectual speculation and new steps forward have been taken either by bold heretics or by mystics, happily emancipated from the constriction of literal dogma. Neo-Platonic mysticism—then still pagan—was a powerful force in the science of the late Roman Empire; in its Christian form it was even more powerful in breaking the watertight system of obsolete knowledge fabricated by the late medieval Schoolmen. Many of the Neo-Platonic mystics of the Reformation period seem unintelligible to us: the writings of Paracelsus, the sixteenth-century Swiss physician, and Jakob Boehme, the mystical shoemaker of seventeenth-century Silesia, can seem to us pure gibberish. But new scientific conceptions tend to spring out of metaphysical visions which they then discard. Isaac Newton and many of his contemporary scientists began as heretical mystics. Isaac Newton himself may have been inspired by the unintelligible Jakob Boehme. Out of the mysticism of the Neo-Platonists and the Quakers the heresy of English deism was born, and deism was the matrix of the Enlightenment of the eighteenth century. And it was Neo-Platonism, again, which inspired the advances in biology at the end of the eighteenth century.

More intelligible to us than Neo-Platonism, but also more heretical, was the most rational of all Reformation heresies, Socinianism. The real founder of Socinianism was Erasmus, who was the first to prove that the only text in the New Testament which could be used as evidence for the doctrine of the Trinity was a late and fraudulent interpolation. He did this in 1516. The Socinians drew the obvious conclusion that God was one, not three, and thus revived, in an uncompromising form but on purely intellectual grounds, the old Arian heresy. They also believed in the complete disestablishment of the Church and in toleration. The established churches—Protestant and Catholic alike—expressed horror at such monstrous ideas, and, between the two, the Socinians had a thin time of it. They found a refuge, first in Poland, then, when the Jesuits came to Poland, in Holland. From

The Dominican order became the chief agent of the Inquisition. This painting by Pedro Berruguete shows its founder, Saint Dominic, presiding over the auto-da-fé of two heretics —although the evidence that he himself ever did is dubious.

Holland, in the seventeenth century, they exercised great influence in England, sometimes even within the Established Church. Whether he was a disciple of Boehme or not, Newton was certainly a Socinian. So was John Locke. In the seventeenth and eighteenth centuries the Socinians were regarded as the intellectual leaders of the English dissenters. Ultimately even the established churches have caught up with them. Since the eighteenth century, Protestants have generally believed that Erasmus was right about the New Testament references to the Trinity. Even the pope has not tried to deny it since 1898. But neither the pope, nor the Archbishop of Canterbury, nor the Lutherans, nor the Calvinists, nor the Greek Orthodox Church has yet come to the more radical "Socinian" conclusion that God is not three but one. That, at this time of day, would be too difficult.

Such is our debt to the long tradition of European heresy. The heretics have been, if not the makers, at least the pacemakers of industrial society, scientific advance, disestablishment of the Church, and religious toleration. But those who prefer orthodoxy can at least make one boast. Heretics have done nothing for art. One reason is no doubt economic. The wealth and patronage which spends itself in art has always been at the disposal of the established church, not of its persecuted critics, and this economic fact has often become a moral attitude: heresy, which is essentially intellectual, disdains appeals to the senses. Moreover, the puritan spirit, which is so powerful in heresy, is positively opposed to art. Magnificent churches, to heretics, have symbolized only the wealth and corruption of the Church, religious pictures have been falsifications of the Gospel, statues have been "dead images," "idols" only fit for destruction. Erasmus, seeing the elaborate Certosa di Pavia, could only exclaim that all that cost might have been spent on the poor. Zwingli, seeing the splendid abbey of Einsiedeln, was roused to hatred of the rich, corrupt church which preferred magnificence and magic to piety and humanity. The English puritans hewed the heads off statues, shivered stained-glass windows, and threw a painting by Rubens into the Thames. The artistic product of two thousand years of heresy is nil. On the other hand, as Gibbon remarked, "the Catholic superstition, which is always the enemy of reason, is often the parent of the arts." Only a rich, established church, which appeals to the senses as well as the conscience, can afford to patronize, or wants to employ, a Giotto, a Fra Angelico, a Greco, or a Rubens.

H. R. Trevor-Roper, a frequent contributor to HORIZON, *is Regius Professor of Modern History at Oxford University.*

m Rhein." They sing the "Loreleï" again as the steamers glide by the humming cities,

at stud this almost excessively romantic landscape. A visit and a personal memory

The Rhine

BY FRANCIS RUSSELL

Of all the great rivers of the world, it is the Rhine that I know best. My almost obsessive feeling of involvement with it has continued ever since my first glimpse of its gray-green waters a third of a century ago. It seemed then—I sensed it even as a schoolboy—more than water flowing; it seemed a river of destiny. For the Rhine flows through the middle of history as surely and as mightily as it flows eight hundred miles, from the Swiss Alps to the Hook of Holland.

From the time of the Romans to the Second World War, it has remained a formidable military obstacle. Once, it divided Roman Gaul from the somber forests of the Germanic tribes, just as centuries later it divided the French and German civilizations. Within its reaches the bloody drama of the Nibelungen saga played itself out. After the Battle of Leipzig, Blücher crossed the Rhine near Kaub—on a pontoon bridge built by Russian troops—to exact the final reckoning from Napoleon. During the interlude between the two world wars the Maginot and Siegfried lines glowered at each other along parts of the river. At Bad Godesberg, across the Rhine from the legendary Drachenfels, Hitler met the umbrella-carrying Chamberlain in 1938, shortly before the Munich Agreement. In the autumn of 1944 the Rhine's swirling current offered a barrier to advancing British and American armies.

Rhenus the Roman legionaries called it, but long before they arrived the Germanic tribes had named their sacred river *Ryn.* The name may have come originally from an Anglo-Saxon word

meaning a stream or ditch, or from *rin,* a Frisian word for "run." But the Romans adapted it to their grammatical forms even as they set their legions' marks on its banks and tamed it with their bridges.

The Limes—Rome's fortified boundary line—extended 342 miles, from Bonn on the Rhine to Regensburg on the Danube. Along the river's banks today Roman names persist: Augst, a few miles above Basel (Basilea), is the site of Augusta Rauracorum (44 B.C.), the earliest Roman stronghold on the river; Bacharach, no doubt because of its vineyards, evolved from *Ara Bacchi* (Altar of Bacchus); Oberwesel was the military station Vosolvia; Coblenz lies at the junction—*Ad Confluentes* —of the Rhine and the Moselle; Andernach was Autunnacum; Cologne, originally named Colonia Claudia Agrippina, in honor of Nero's mother, was known among the Romans as Colonia.

"Descending from the summits of the Rhaetian Alps," was the way in which the Romans described the river's beginnings. The Vorder Rhine originates among the stones and mountain shadows of Lake Toma, and then flows with a rush into the isolation of the Vorder Rhine Valley (where the spoken language is still the Latin-derived Romansh). The second principal headstream, the Hinter Rhine, is born of a glacier in the Rheinwaldhorn, highest of the Adula Alp summits, and emerges as a mountain stream, light-green and boisterous, into the quiet of the level Rheinwald Valley. Below the valley it again becomes turbulent as it is joined by a tributary, the Averser Rhine. At the insig-

The Rhine (near Kaub):
"A blending of all beauties,—streams and dells,
Fruit, foliage, crag, wood, corn-field, mountain, vine,
And chiefless castles breathing stern farewells."
–Byron, Childe Harold

nificant valley town of Reichenau, each forty miles from its source, the two branches conjoin and become at last the Rhine.

Past Chur the waters are swift and icy as they flow to divide Switzerland from Austria and Liechtenstein, but it is as a shallow, muddied stream that the Rhine finally reaches the German border at Lake Constance. This deep lake, forty-six miles long and eleven miles across at its widest point, was known as Lacus Brigantinus in the days when it reflected the beaked Roman galleys. On its shores are three German towns of importance: Lindau, Friedrichshafen, and Constance. Lindau, the island city, was the base of the Roman lake fleet. Friedrichshafen became noted only in modern times as the launching point of Count Zeppelin's dirigible in 1900. Later a more advanced Zeppelin took off from here on the first round-the-world flight. Constance is most noted historically as the meeting place of the 1414 Council where, in the presence of the Holy Roman Emperor Sigismund, three rival popes were deposed, Martin V elected to replace them, and John Hus—in spite of his Imperial safe-conduct—was burned at the stake for heresy.

Filtered of its muddiness by Lake Constance, the Rhine runs west, emerging with new strength and all its former glacial clarity at the bridge linking Eschenz and Stein. Below Schaffhausen, whose falls have been made famous by romantic painters, it becomes a border river, and at Basel, fifty-six miles farther on, turns north at the French frontier. Here the river enters the Rhine Rift and becomes, at last, the fatherland river, the legendary stream leading to Strasbourg, Mannheim, Mainz, and beyond to Bonn, Cologne, Holland, and the North Sea.

Switzerland, Germany, and France meet at Basel in a point on the river called the Three Nations Corner. Basel is a wide, clean, sober Swiss city that, like Geneva, bears the indelible stamp of the Reformation. Even its ancient cathedral, part Romanesque, part Gothic, where Bernard of Clairvaux preached the Second Crusade, is Protestant now. Behind the cathedral is a long terrace with a view across the river to the Black Forest. Seen from here the Rhine gives an impression of concealed strength and depth, and has a cold green color that suggests its glacial origins. Basel is the city of Dürer and Holbein. Erasmus taught there, and in 1526 reported that "everybody understands Latin and Greek, many even Hebrew." Below Basel, the Rhine takes a sharp bend northward and enters the Upper Rhenish Low Plain. This is a rift valley, almost two hundred miles long and up to thirty miles wide, lying between the heights of the Vosges and the Haardt in the west and the Black Forest and the Nibelungen-haunted Odenwald in the east. Most of the valley lies in Alsace on the west bank of the Rhine. In Roman times, this long stretch of river was the boundary between Gaul and Germania. Louis XIV, having conquered Alsace, is said to

have looked down at the valley from Mount St. Odile, and called it "my fair garden."

This part of the Rhine is wide and placid, flowing past poplar-edged banks through a flat, somewhat monotonous landscape. Storks, the token birds of Alsace, gather to fish in the many marshes. Strasbourg, though actually two miles from the Rhine, seems as organically linked with the river as it does with Alsace. The city has a paradoxical charm, as border cities often do, for it is French in fact and feeling, yet German in appearance and tradition.

The soaring spire of the Strasbourg cathedral, seen from every angle of the countryside, is a symbol of Alsace. During the French Revolution, a committee of Jacobins, after installing a Goddess of Reason in the cathedral, decided to pull down the spire because they felt its dominance of the landscape violated the principle of democratic equality. The actual dismantling, however, presented a formidable engineering task. Finally, as a compromise, a giant tin liberty cap, painted red, was placed over it.

No one who has read Goethe's autobiographical *Truth and Poetry* can visit Strasbourg without picturing the young Goethe arriving there, in 1770, and hurrying at once to visit the cathedral. A Colossus, he called it, and admired it greatly, even though its Gothic style was, at the moment, quite out of fashion. A few weeks later in the Rhine village of Sesenheim, twenty miles north of Strasbourg, the elegant young student met and fell in love with blue-eyed Friederike Brion, a pastor's daughter, and was inspired by this love to write his "Sesenheim lyrics." With these poems, which introduced a personal, lyric note for the first time since the minnesingers, modern German poetry begins. Goethe's friend Herder had rediscovered the German past in the folk songs he was then collecting; Goethe in his Sesenheim lyrics focused this consciousness on the present. The awareness of Germany as an entity, the Gothic heritage, German nationalism with all its greatness and the depths of its somber tragedy, were born in that Strasbourg springtime. The poems mark a unique moment in the German spirit.

The red-roofed city that saw the origins of German nationalism also saw within its walls the emergence of revolutionary French nationalism. It was the home of two French generals, Kléber and Kellermann; and here, in 1792, Rouget de Lisle wrote the "Song of the Army of the Rhine," which he sang for the first time before the Mayor of Strasbourg and which finally became known as the Marseillaise.

It is sixty-five miles downstream to Speyer, on the German side of the river, with always the line of the Black Forest to the east. Once the capital of a Roman province, Speyer is a small, unremarkable manufacturing city noted principally for its Romanesque cathedral. Built on the foundations of a Roman

*At Rheinfelden, a cozy Swiss village
near Basel, the Rhine forms the
border between Switzerland and Germany.*

CHARLES ROTKIN

temple, this is Germany's largest Romanesque church. Eight German emperors lie buried in its crypt. The cathedral was burned by Louis XIV's forces and again by French Revolutionary troops. For a time the ruins were used as a powder magazine, and the cathedral was not rededicated until 1822. In Speyer there is a famous wine museum, its most popular exhibit a third-century Roman bottle still filled with its original wine (or so it is claimed).

There is nothing ancient about the humming industrial center of Mannheim, chief port of navigation of the middle Rhine, a dozen miles below Speyer. The regularity of the streets stems from the baroque town planning carried out by the Elector Charles Philip in the eighteenth century. Here the Neckar meets the Rhine; perhaps the most interesting thing that can be said of the Elector's city is that Heidelberg is not far away. But at an equal distance beyond Mannheim, history renews itself at Worms. As Wormatia it was the seat of the Merovingian kings. Earlier, it was the court of the Burgundians, where Siegfried won Kriemhild. Across the Rhine, in the dark reaches of the Odenwald, Hagen the killer tracked Siegfried through the beechwoods and ran him through with his spear. Charlemagne occasionally kept his court at Worms. In 1521 Luther defended his thesis of the Reformed doctrine before the emperor Charles V at the Diet of Worms—that event so punningly familiar to generations of English-speaking schoolboys.

Thirty-five miles farther on at Mainz, the next large city

(once called "the golden" because of its riches, and today the capital of Rhineland Palatinate), the Rhine turns west again, flowing steadily, now a half mile wide. Mainz is remembered for Saint Boniface, the Apostle of the Germans and the city's first archbishop, and for Johann Gensfleisch (goose flesh) who under the more resounding name of Gutenberg invented the printing press.

At Mainz, and the spa of Wiesbaden almost across the river from it, the Rheingau begins—a castle-studded landscape of sharp hills, flashing water, and villages that seem to be half-drowsing in a dream of the Middle Ages. Here is the great wine-growing country marked by slopes patterned with vineyards. On the way to Bingen the massed buildings of Schloss Johannisberg, built by the prince-abbots of Fulda, glower several hundred feet above the river. At Rüdesheim there are wine cellars cut deep into layers of subterranean rock. Each river town and village has its wine festival in the autumn and crowns its wine queen.

Winkel, near the eastern end of the Rheingau, too small a village to appear on any of the larger maps, was the home of the eighteenth-century poet Clemens Brentano, and here, in their medieval house, Clemens and his sister Bettina gathered a literary circle around them. Clemens wrote poems and sang them, accompanying himself on his guitar, to music of his own composing. Bettina—who at twenty-two had a literary affair with the fifty-eight-year-old Goethe—married Achim von Arnim,

21

St. Goarshausen, seen from a Rhine steamer on a rainy day. Burg Katz, on the hill, looks north to Burg Maus (not shown).

Clemens's collaborator on the most famous of German folk-song collections, *Des Knaben Wunderhorn.* At Winkel, Clemens wrote the first poem about the Lorelei. In their letters and stories and poems the members of the Brentano circle wrote and sang about the Rhine and created its image as the symbolic German river. Without them Wagner would never have written his *Ring* cycle in the form that he did; perhaps he might never have composed the *Ring*'s sword motif, which Hitler said was ringing in his ears during the sinister weeks of September, 1939.

The legend of Father Rhine reached its culmination in the throbbing measures of "The Watch on the Rhine" and in the ponderous Niederwald Monument, which, topped by a heroic figure of Germania, has dominated the town of Rüdesheim since the last quarter of the nineteenth century. The legend dissolved in the chaotic end of World War II, leaving the Rhine as a great artery of Europe but no longer equated with a Reich or fatherland. How thoroughly it dissolved is apparent at the Niederwald Monument, on any holiday afternoon, in the scoffing incredulity with which younger German tourists read the pompous patriotic verses from "The Watch on the Rhine" that are carved on the monument's base.

At Bingen the Rhine turns north abruptly, to enter a deep gorge, with the Taunus and later the Westerwald bounding it on the east and the Hunsrück on the west. The stream becomes more turbulent as it narrows from a sixth of a mile to just a few hundred feet at the Lorelei Rock. From here to Cologne is the most picturesque part of all, a legendary countryside of jagged cliffs and purple-distance hills and ancient towns huddled below ruined castles. It is the Rhine as conceived by the tourist who has never been there, as perpetuated on a thousand scenic postcards, as hailed by the excursion-steamer passengers who sing the "Lorelei" as they pass the sheer rock where she sat, above the swirling current opposite St. Goar. It is also the part of Germany that has touched me most deeply. I came to know it first in the summer of 1931, one of Germany's crisis years, when I arrived as a schoolboy at the Village of Biebernheim in the hills above St. Goar to live with a Lutheran pastor who was a relative of my mother's godmother—and learn German. Since then I have seen the Rhine through the slits of a Canadian armored car in the spring attack of 1945, in the hunger days of the Allied occupation, and again in the renewed abundance of the West German Republic's *Wirtschaftswunder.* Over the years the region has become so much a part of me that I cannot imagine being the self that I am without having known it.

On my first journey to Biebernheim, coming from Rotterdam, I somehow managed to take the wrong train and had to spend the night at Cologne. The next day, Sunday, while waiting until late afternoon for the Rheingold Express, I wandered along the west bank of the Rhine past the cathedral. In spite of the gathering crisis, deceptively perhaps, everybody looked bright and happy. Mothers were pushing fat little children in gocarts, fathers following behind smoking their after-dinner cigars. Down the Rhine, paddling with the current, came a succession

of tanned young couples in the new folding skiffs, called *falt-booten*. I found the Rhine itself a little disappointing. Somehow I had expected it to be turbulent—at least wider than it was.

The paths along the banks were littered with the papers and handbills of some new political party that had just been launched the day before. That afternoon I saw my first swastika pin, in the lapel of a young man who also sported a green Tyrolean hat with a goat's beard stuck in the band at the back. The porter at the hotel near the station had a pair of swastika cuff links.

I arrived at Biebernheim after dark. Nobody met me, and I climbed the twisting road past Ruin Rheinfels all alone under a warm, starry sky. I found the parsonage without trouble, having been told that it had a boulder and a great linden in front of it and was the only house in the village with an iron gate. One entered it from the street level, going through a long corridor hung with the braided straw wreaths of former harvests and passing a low-ceilinged kitchen where, when I first went by, a girl of about fourteen with long Gretchen braids sat peeling apples by the stove. The dining room, upstairs, was the main room of the house, sunny and warm with low windows opening on a porch twined over with Virginia creeper. In the center was a heavy circular table, about which we stood for a moment before each meal, holding hands all round while the pastor said grace: there were the Frau Pastor; Notburg, the shy red-haired daughter; Hans and Werner, two towheaded boys who boarded there and took the train each day to Boppard where they were *Unterprimaners* at the Gymnasium; the pastor; and myself.

After grace, the pastor nodded and took his napkin from the heavy silver ring that had "Head of the House" engraved on it. This was the signal for the rest of us to begin eating. I can still see his bearded patriarchal face as he sat at the head of the table, the deep lines in his forehead accented by the lamplight. After the meal, he would read to us from some local and forgotten imitator of Sir Walter Scott, while the boys fidgeted and I struggled to comprehend the language. The old man could be stern, too. Hans's one dream was of the glory of being a soldier. Secretly (although I think Notburg knew it), he was a member of the Hitler Youth. Since he felt that soldiers should know how to ride, he would sometimes borrow a peasant's dray horse and practice bareback in the lower meadow, to come home stinking of the stable. Once a week he would steal away to drill with the local Storm Troopers, led by the blacksmith. He never dared let the pastor know about this, or about his Nazi sympathies; but one evening, because Werner had teased him, he came to the table wearing a small swastika in his buttonhole. We held hands as usual, but before the pastor took his napkin from the ring, he looked at Hans and then boomed out in his sternest pulpit voice: "No one may wear that un-Christian emblem at my table. Leave the room!" Hans stood up, bowed to the pastor, and walked out.

Biebernheim itself—with its uneven, half-timbered houses huddled like a brood of chickens about the church, whose baroque, onion-shaped tower was topped by a chanticleer—had not changed in two hundred years. No car or bicycle dared the ruts of its main street, where children played and ducks wad-

23

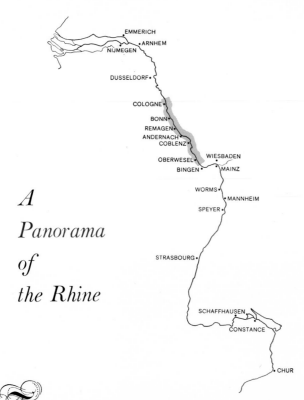

*A
Panorama
of
the Rhine*

The pictorial map of the Rhine that appears as a supplement to this issue of HORIZON is reproduced from one published for tourists in 1842. At that time thousands of ladies and gentlemen from France, England, and America were flocking to the Rhine; and with this map in one hand and a spyglass in the other, they sat on the awninged decks of paddle wheelers and watched the castles go by. It was comfortable travel: snacks, such as a *Bifstek mit Bratkartoffeln,* were available all day, and Rhine wine flowed like Rhine water. At night the voyagers trooped ashore to well-appointed inns, the best in Europe. The only railroad in this vicinity was a forty-mile track from Cologne to Aachen; but travel by post coach (our map notes departure points) was not arduous, since Rhineside roads were macadamized. And even the most fragile lady tourist could be hoisted to a castle summit, in a sort of chair strapped to a small donkey. Victor Hugo, who journeyed from Cologne to Mainz in 1843, had only one complaint: "the stranger is obliged to have his hand in constant communion with his pocket." For example, while dining one day at St. Goar, Hugo heard guns being fired off so that tourists could enjoy the fifteen-times echo; whereupon, a waiter passed a plate and each, says Hugo, "paid for his echo."

By 1842 Prussia had gobbled up most of the area shown on our map, but the castles and country houses were still owned by hereditary *Prinzen, Grafen, Barone,* and *Freiherren,* who, despite lip service to Prussia, ruled their peasants with an autocratic hand and caused many of them to exchange this bucolic landscape for America. From Lake Constance to the sea, the only bridges over the Rhine were made of moored barges (our map shows one at Cologne and another at Coblenz). A common but amazing sight on the river was an enormous raft, up to 900 feet long, made of logs that had been cut on the upper Rhine and were being floated to the sea. Four to five hundred men rowed such a raft, and their families and livestock were also aboard, creating a floating town.

Near the top of our map, the Cologne cathedral is shown as it looked then, forlorn and unfinished, with a disused crane atop one tower; so it had stood for about two hundred years. Soon after, collections were taken up (once more the tourist's hand was in communion with his pocket), and work recommenced. The final stone was placed in 1880.

dled. There was a slow, eighteenth-century rhythm to each lingering day that suggested the Sesenheim of Goethe's lost Friederike. But the solemn Notburg would scarcely have made a Friederike; and, as a modern touch, there was Hans.

On Thursdays and Fridays the pastor studied, and wrote his sermon, and on Saturday everyone prepared for Sunday. But on the other weekdays he often took me with him on walks to the little Rhine towns and villages or sometimes to neighboring parsonages hidden in the solitary folds of the hills. We followed the upland paths above the river, sometimes going as far south as Bingen, past Oberwesel and Bacharach, and sometimes north as far as Boppard. And as we walked in the transparent early autumn afternoons, the old man told me the history and legends of the castles and ruins we passed. Others I learned from *The Most Beautiful Legends of the Rhine,* a little book I bought to help me learn the language. Ruin Rheinfels—once the largest castle fortress on the Rhine—had been gutted by the French in 1793. Until then it had been owned by the Landgraves of Hesse-Cassel, one of whom is remembered in American history for selling his subjects, the Hessians, to fight for the British in the Revolution. From my bedroom window I could see across the river to the round tower and castellations of Burg Katz, built in 1393 by the counts of Katzenellenbogen (Cat's Elbow). The counts derisively called the castle on the next peak north, which belonged to the Archbishop of Trier, Burg Maus. Cat and Mouse were the first two things I saw each morning.

After I had finished my Rhine legends, I read Heine's fragment that is perhaps his masterpiece, *The Rabbi of Bacharach.* For a beginner like myself the German was much too hard, but the pastor read it with me, and gradually the tale emerged in all its shuddering grimness. The pastor had an old volume of Delkeskamp's *Panorama of The Rhine,* and would point out each place in the book to me before we went there. We visited Bacharach several times, in those long-drawn-out, utterly quiet afternoons when the peasants were harvesting potatoes on the uplands. For miles around, the smoke from the smoldering root fires rose straight and undeviating in the windless air. There was one point where the path dipped down near a patch of scabiosa, and there, below us, we caught our first glimpse of the rose-red walls and the involuted tracery of the Werner Chapel, one of the most delicately contrived examples of German late-Gothic. That enchanting ruin, according to the pastor, was consecrated to Saint Werner, the alleged victim in another of those cruel fantastic legends of Jewish ritual murder such as Heine had used in his tale.

Sometimes on such drowsy afternoons I would wander by myself past Ruin Rheinfels down the road lined with horse chestnut trees, take the ferry across the Rhine from St. Goar to St. Goarshausen, and climb the valley road behind the sprawled-out town to the summit of the Lorelei Rock. As I sat on the lookout in the lingering warmth of the old wives' summer, everything seemed so enduringly peaceful. Below me the excursion steamers, churning the current into white froth, looked no larger than toys. So quiet it was that I could hear the passengers singing Heine's familiar "Lorelei" as they passed the cliff, a custom that Hitler, soon afterward, forebade.

Tranquillity was, of course, a deception, even in Biebernheim. Whenever the Storm Troopers met in the inn, Zur Linde, almost opposite the church, their voices rang out harshly through the night. For a long time the pastor had been denouncing the Nazis from the pulpit, and now some of the villagers began to boycott his Sunday services.

I left Biebernheim early in November, on an overcast morning that had a trace of snow in the air. As I stood for the last time in the shelter of the parsonage doorway, I noticed that someone had daubed a swastika on the boulder beside the gate. Notburg was scrubbing it off with a brush and hot water. She looked up at me and smiled, then went on with her scrubbing.

Although I had planned to come back the following summer, I was not to see the Rhine again until late in the autumn of 1944, when I came to Holland as a soldier. A few miles beyond the Dutch border the Rhine splits in two. The larger branch— renamed the Waal—flows through Nijmegen, and the smaller —the Lower Rhine—passes to the north at Arnhem. At Nijmegen I found a low, sad landscape, like no part of the Rhineland I had been familiar with, and made the more forlorn by the patchy winter and by the wrecked skeletons of gliders and tanks from the foiled September attack. The 82nd U.S. Airborne Division had managed to seize the southern end of the Nijmegen bridge, and the 504th Parachute Regiment then crossed the four hundred yards of water in assault boats, to secure the northern side, under a German fire that turned the water red as it had been at the time of Caesar and of the Nibelungs. The Guards of the British 8th Armored Brigade had cleared the bridge itself. But the aftermath was an anticlimax for us—that long winter's wait, the tedium broken by an occasional shell or buzz bomb or the ephemeral flurry caused by the capture of a one-man midget submarine. From the bridge a causeway led northward to German-held Arnhem ten miles away, a no man's land of dike-meshed fields. On the horizon south of Nijmegen I could see the low hills across the border in Germany. Were my old friends still there, or perhaps even closer, at Arnhem? Somehow I never could quite imagine them as enemies.

In February we moved forward, over the German border, along the west bank of the Rhine, and into the bloody maze of the Reichswald. I crossed the Rhine on a motorcycle over a pontoon bridge at Emmerich, near the Dutch border, feeling so exultant at crossing the river again that I promptly drove into a ditch. Several Germans helped me out. Emmerich was the most smashed place I was ever to see, for in fact there was nothing left, not a building, not even a solitary wall. I passed through Arnhem the day after it was liberated. Orange banners were fluttering from every window, and civilians clapped as we passed. In front of the German Soldiers' Cinema, the old posters were still on display: "All This Week. *I Love You Best.*"

Often in those climactic months I thought of Biebernheim.

Whatever had happened, I felt I wanted to see the old parsonage once again. But it was not until almost a year later that I managed to get to the Rhineland from Hildesheim where I had been assigned as political intelligence officer with the British 30th Corps. At the gray end of a December afternoon, under a sallow sky streaked in the west with saffron, I came once more to Cologne. From the Autobahn some miles away, the silhouette of the twin-towered cathedral loomed up, a reassuring bulk against the sunset. At that distance the structure looked intact, although a closer inspection made me doubt whether the shattered fabric could ever be restored. Suddenly as I reached the bank of the Rhine the cathedral's great Emperor Bell began to strike, a burring resonance that echoed consolingly above the miles of surrounding ruins, like a Christmas message.

Those ruins seemed to have no limits. All Cologne's streets by the railway station where I had arrived so long ago were obliterated by several stories of rubble. Paths like goat tracks traversed the heaps. There were no street lights, no public services in this shell of a city. At night it was as dark as it must have been in the medieval town. And just as then, slops were thrown with a warning shout from the upper windows of the few remaining houses.

I stayed overnight at a British mess, then next morning drove in my jeep along the west bank of the Rhine towards Biebernheim. Bonn, the old university town, lay in a mist. It had begun to rain by the time I reached Coblenz, a ghost city, unroofed, the standing walls without substance. Through a gap of smashed buildings I found myself looking down on the juncture of the Rhine and the Moselle known as the German Corner. There a heroic statue of William I had stood until the final air attack, and now lay unhorsed in a shattered pile of masonry. Above the bleak garrison fortress of Ehrenbreitstein on top of the sheer cliff opposite, where the Kaiser's regiments once drilled, hung a French tricolor.

Beyond Coblenz the road ran between the riverbank and the steep skeletal vineyards; and under each shelter of overhanging cliff, groups of refugees, raw-faced and miserable, clustered about fires they had kindled from sticks and rubbish, stretching out their hands to the meager blaze. The mist obscured the hills and castles, and I could see little more than the occasional orange glow of the wayside fires and the glistening, uneven line of pavement ahead of me, clammy with rotted leaves.

Boppard, where Hans and Werner had been students at the Gymnasium, still looked familiar even though many of the half-timbered houses sagged on their cracked foundations and the straw hung in wisps from the broken roof tiles; then came other towns, increasingly familiar to me until, just as the early twilight bore down, I saw the white stone houses of St. Goar and the mist-shrouded silhouette of Ruin Rheinfels.

I spun my jeep up the hill, and Biebernheim lay before me in the darkness like a dream. The church and the old overhanging houses were unaltered, the boulder and the linden still shared the space before the parsonage. Perhaps, I thought as I walked up the path, the old man had died, for he would be long

WILLIAM OLCOTT

past eighty now. I felt my footsteps hesitate. But tacked to the door was the customary sheet of paper with the names of all the occupants, their ages and their callings—as required by the occupation authorities. "Pfarrer Velthusen, aged 85" was written in rather crabbed German across the top line, but the German *Pfarrer* had been crossed out and the French *Pasteur* inserted above it. The rest I did not bother to read, for in that glimpse I saw that my journey back in time had not been in vain.

When I first knew the pastor, his eyes had been like old Von Hindenburg's, narrowly slit in folds of flesh. Now, in his advanced age, they had opened wide and were surprisingly blue, like the eyes of a child. He came into the familiar dining room with a heavy, dragging walk, leaning on Notburg's arm. He wore thick knee-length felt boots, and his thin white hair straggled in tufts over the collar of his ancient frock coat. I realized that he was moved by my visit, but he could not seem to find words to say so after his first greeting. Notburg had become a middle-aged woman with lifeless red hair. She had married, and her five-year-old boy was with her, but her husband was still a prisoner in the American zone.

I brought out some instant coffee, Notburg heated water, and we once more sat round the table. The dining room, smelling faintly of drains, had become shabby. Water had stained the walls, the curtains were gone and so was the carpet, and the deal boards lay exposed. As the pastor sipped his coffee, watching me in silence, and the boy sat by the oven playing with some potatoes put there to dry, Notburg and I talked of the past. Al-

most at once I asked about Hans and Werner. "They are dead," she said. "You are the only one left." Hans, who had so wanted to be a soldier, got his wish. He fought at Stalingrad, and there he vanished, even to his name, in that anonymous slaughter, for no one had ever heard of him again. Werner's fate was even more ironic. "You didn't know it then," Notburg told me, "but he was a half-Jew. His parents came from South Africa, the part that used to be the German southwest. When Hitler came to power, Father told Werner he should go back to South Africa, that Germany was no place for him. He didn't want to go, said Germany was his country and that was where he wanted to stay. But Father wrote Werner's mother and made him leave before it was too late. When the war came, he joined the South African Air Force. He was shot down over Germany."

My last visit to the Rhineland was in the autumn of 1962, in the fat, somewhat blatant prosperity of the West German Republic. The flotsam of the war, which had seemed so permanent in 1945, had been swept away. Even in Cologne, which I had thought shattered beyond mending, one had to have a sharp eye to discover any traces of the famous thousand-plane attacks. During the war, when an air-raid shelter was being dug near the cathedral, a Roman mosaic of the second century, once the floor of a villa banqueting hall, was unearthed. Eighty yards square, it portrays the legend of Dionysus and is one of the most splendid mosaics ever uncovered. The site is now a museum.

Sharp eyes are not enough in Düsseldorf, for in this elegant

26

In Holland the Rhine divides into several branches, of which the Lek (right) is the most northerly.

city poised between Cologne and Holland every trace of the war has long since vanished. This is Germany's most cosmopolitan city, looking more to Paris and London than to Bonn or Berlin. Here, where prosperity truly glitters, a Mercedes is known as a Ruhr Volkswagen. Along the double width of the shaded Königsallee, the heart of Düsseldorf, the prosperity becomes tangible in the once-more-plump, middle-aged Germans taking their afternoon coffee with cream tarts. In Düsseldorf is Germany's first skyscraper, the sleek rectangle of the Phoenix-Rheinrohr building. It would dwarf a dozen cathedrals.

It was from Düsseldorf this time that I started out along the familiar route south, past civil-service Bonn with its concentric rings of new villas and its bare white parliament building on the Rhine bank, and on to Coblenz where I stopped for lunch. Coblenz, too, had healed the wounds that had seemed mortal. At the German Corner only the plinth remained where the bronze William I had pranced on his horse. I thought the bare stone base an improvement. Fortress Ehrenbreitstein, across the river, had become a museum and a youth hostel.

Biebernheim in another afternoon's quiet was for me merely a passing detour, although the placid moment that greeted me could have been that of a third of a century before. But the pastor had been dead these ten years, Notburg and her husband had gone to West Berlin, and the links with the past were broken. I drove a few hundred yards beyond the village and stopped to look back. Biebernheim seemed to be asleep in the long slanting light, the red-tiled roofs giving off the faintest shimmer of heat waves, swallows circling above the bulbous slate church tower with its chanticleer. I could not see the blue ribbon of the Rhine, but the Mouse and the Cat were clear before me, and beyond the harvest fields and the checkered vineyards, to the right, the Lorelei summit shimmered in its greenery. Eastward wave after wave of bluish hills receded into a distance that seemed infinite. Here the quintessence of romantic landscape still endured. Moritz von Schwind or Hans Thoma would have set up their palettes and painted the scene with delight. Any modern painter, however, would have turned away in disgust. The landscape was just too picturesquely perfect, as if actuality itself had been faked. Middle-class Germans who now settled for a print of Van Gogh's sunflowers in their living rooms would reject any reproduction of what I saw in front of me as pure kitsch.

For art even as for history, the Rhine's formidable tradition was dead. Europe had become too close-knit for any Germanic river of destiny. The Rhine was once again merely a flow of water, and a tourist's stream at that. No men's choir would ever again march in fancy to "The Watch on the Rhine." That song had echoed ominously for the last time as Hitler strode in triumph through Strasbourg Cathedral in 1940. Even the Biebernheimers in their remoteness had accepted the change and the future. From almost every ancient red-tiled roof I could see the glittering metal wand of a television antenna.

Francis Russell, a New Englander, writes on many subjects— from Sacco and Vanzetti (Tragedy in Dedham) *to movies. He is currently at work on a biography of Warren G. Harding.*

Can reason and logic solve all of man's problems? The great Roman poet Lucretius seems to take the affirmative side in man's unending debate on this question— but his verses are charged with agonizing doubts

LUCR

The material of the world is not what it seems to be. A solid, like rock, or a fluid, like water, is only apparently solid or fluid. Both the rock and the water are composed of myriads of invisible particles which are associated by laws of their own and are in constant movement.

This earth and the sun and moon and planets, all our universe, in fact, is made up of atoms. The atoms came together to form them, as tiny drops of water come together to form a huge river. In time the atoms will separate again, and our universe will cease to exist, as a river does when it runs into the desert and evaporates. But the atoms will never cease to exist. They, and they alone, are eternal.

Earthquakes, volcanic eruptions, epidemics, and such disasters are not caused by God's anger. They are natural phenomena and can be explained scientifically.

Sensation and thought are functions of the body. The soul is not immortal, but is born in the body, develops with it, and will cease to exist when the other physical functions, such as respiration and heartbeat, stop.

Of these four propositions, most civilized people in the Western world nowadays believe the first and the third. Many believe the second. Some believe the fourth. All four were accepted as unquestionable truth by many Greeks and Romans; they became the theme of a magnificent Latin poem; they were maintained for at least five centuries; and thereafter, for a thousand years, they were buried in oblivion. The first and second, if anyone had even thought of them in the Middle Ages, would have been dismissed as ridiculous; the third and fourth as blasphemous. And yet the Latin poem built on these statements somehow survived. That such a book, opposed to all the tenets of medieval Christianity and common sense, should have been laboriously copied out in the ninth century, obviously by monks who understood some of what they read and transcribed, is truly surprising. The poem itself, and the character of its author, are something of a mystery, too. But one thing is certain: it is a superb poem and it was written by a great poet. His name was Lucretius. He wrote it about sixty years before the birth of Jesus, and he called it *The Nature of Things*, i.e., *The Nature of the Universe*.

Who Lucretius was, where he lived, how he learned (or taught himself) to write so well, who his friends were, and even what social status he held, we have no way of knowing. None of his contemporaries ever mentions him by name— except Cicero, who remarks that his poetry is full not only of genius but also of technical skill, and Nepos, who refers

NATIONAL GALLERY, LONDON

Botticelli's *Mars and Venus* (left) is believed to
have been inspired by these invocatory lines
from Lucretius's poem *The Nature of the Universe:*

Kind lady Venus, cause the savage work of war
to rest in calm surcease throughout the sea and land.
For you, and you alone, can bless mankind with quiet
peace: all the savage work of war is ruled by Mars
the warrior, who often sinks upon your breast
a helpless victim of the quenchless wound of love;
with supple neck supine, he gazes up to you,
feasting his greedy eyes and drinking in your beauty,
a captive hanging helpless on your breathing lips.
Embrace him with your sacred body, lady Venus,
and while he lies enraptured, speak sweet pleading words
beseeching him to grant the Romans rest and peace.

ETIUS

BY GILBERT HIGHET

in passing to his death. Several centuries later, in a historical survey, a sort of World Almanac, Saint Jerome states
that Lucretius was born in 94 B.C. and died at the age of
forty-three; another late writer places his death in 55 B.C.,
but the discrepancy is small. He was evidently about a dozen
years younger than Julius Caesar and more than twenty
years older than Virgil. This agrees, also, with the historical
allusions in his poem. Clearly he lived through many of the
desperate wars and revolutionary outbreaks that devastated
the Roman world in the early first century before Christ,
and died not long before they came to their climax in
Caesar's successful attack on the republic. He speaks of himself as a Roman born and bred; obviously he was well educated in literature and philosophy, both Latin and Greek;
probably he was a gentleman of independent means and re-
tiring nature; certainly he was a genius.

Lucretius did not invent the doctrines that are the body
of his poem. What he did was to clothe them in noble verse
of a power and subtlety previously unknown in Latin, devise lucid and eloquent illustrations for them, and infuse
them with such a perfectly unmistakable and all but irresistible personal emotion that he often seems—over the gulf
of time and through the barrier of language—to speak di-

rectly to us from heart to heart. The poetry is his. The doctrines are those of Epicurus.

Epicurus was an Athenian schoolmaster's son who founded
a philosophical college in Athens in 306 B.C., and taught his
own system of philosophy quietly and successfully there for
nearly forty years. It was not merely a place of instruction,
but a community of friends. Although Epicurus was a pro-
digiously energetic writer, the center of his school was not
thought of as the library, but as the garden; and perhaps
the Hindu word *ashram* would best describe the serenity and
dedication of the place. Although he was a mild, pure-hearted
man, his name has become the Hebrew word for an unbe-
liever or renegade, *apikoros*; and although he was scru-
pulously moderate in diet and called a pot of cheese a luxuri-
ous treat, an "epicure" in English and French is a devoted
gourmet like Brillat-Savarin.

Epicurus claimed to have originated his entire philosophy,
but he owed much to his predecessors. The theory that the
physical universe is composed of an infinite number of vari-
ously shaped atoms constantly moving in void space was
worked out a century before his birth by two brilliant philosophical thinkers, Leucippus and his pupil Democritus. By
anticipating some of the most advanced scientific discoveries

29

of our own era, and by doing so without complex apparatus, almost wholly through pure speculative reasoning, these two men gave one of those demonstrations of penetrating and comprehensive thought that justify us in calling the Greeks the founders of Western civilization.

Epicurus took their description of the structure of matter and united it with ethical, psychological, social, and religious teachings of his own. Among the four propositions stated at the beginning of this article, Leucippus and Democritus enunciated the first and second; they would have accepted the third and fourth, and perhaps they actually set them down, although their books are now lost. But it was Epicurus who built all four into a coherent system which, with its many ramifications and its subtle analyses, claimed to solve all the important problems of the world, and in particular to show mankind the secret of true happiness.

The secret, Epicurus maintained, was easy to understand. Only mental sloth, or superstition, or timidity, or evil custom kept everyone from grasping it. It could be stated in a series of interlocking propositions, and, memorized, could become an ever-present guide through life. Its basis was . . . but let Lucretius explain it.

The terror and the darkness in the mind must yield
not to the sun or to the glittering shafts of day
but to the knowledge and analysis of nature.
Now, first, the great initial principle is this:
nothing is made from nothing by the power of God.
This is the fear that grips the hearts of all mankind:
many events they see on earth and in the sky
and cannot understand the causes there at work:
so therefore they believe the will of God controls them.

The second principle corresponds to this. As nothing is created out of nothing,

so further, nature causes all things to dissolve
into their atoms, but does not annihilate them.
The atoms are immortal, indestructible,
and so they cannot ever be obliterated.
No thing can be reduced to nothing; every thing
reverts by dissolution to the basic atoms.

Having laid down this double principle, Lucretius (following the lost work of his master, Epicurus) goes on to give arguments to support it and to demonstrate how it explains many of the phenomena that puzzle minds untrained in logic and science. Sensation, perception, thought, and such psychical events as dreams and visions—he explains them all. But although most of his analysis is scientific, his purpose lies beyond pure science. The real beauty of Epicureanism, he repeats again and again, is that it sets us free from the two great fears: fear of God and fear of death. It does not deny the existence of a divinity. There *are* gods, superhuman in power, supernal in beauty, but they exist far away from our world, illimitably far. Since they are perfectly happy, they do not busy themselves with interfering in mundane affairs: they do not slash the earth with a trident to cause earthquakes, or hurl the thunderbolts that sometimes hit their own temples, or send epidemic diseases among their worshipers. Nor do they answer prayers; nor even hear prayers. We can honor them; we need not fear them. We know of their existence only through visions. They themselves know nothing of our world, and exist far off in outer space.

There are the dwellings of the gods, remote, serene,
which never windblasts shake, or darkling tempests
  drench
with rain, or cold gray crystal snow and freezing hail
besmirch, but always in a cloudless firmament
poised, they remain in spacious smiling radiance.

And death? It is this fear, the greatest of all human fears, that is the most central and most urgent theme of Lucretius's poem. Again and again with passionate emphasis he explains that death is nothing to be feared because it means —nothingness. It is cessation. A man fears death, he explains, because he illogically thinks of himself as *being* the dead corpse that is put away in the ground or burned to ashes on the pyre. But this is absurd. When the functions of life cease, sensation and thought come to an end, total and final. The body dissolves into dust and then into primordial atoms— and where is the man? He is where he was a thousand years before his birth.

Consider how the ages of eternal time
meant nothing to us while we did not yet exist.
This is a mirror held for us by nature, showing
all that the future means after we meet our death.
Is any horror there, or any sense of sadness?
Is it not all as peaceful and as calm as sleep?

As for hell and its torments—all that is an old wives' tale. Or rather, it is a projection of this life. Sisyphus, rolling the huge stone forever up the mountain and doomed to see it roll back, exemplifies insatiate ambition. The Danaides, condemned to draw water in leaky vessels, are those restless spirits who in this life constantly seek for pleasures and are never satisfied. Cerberus, and the Furies, and the demons of punishment—they exist, but they are the torments of fear and remorse that the guilty suffer in this existence, which is for each of us the only one. Therefore, be tranquil. Enjoy your life, which nature has made so pleasant; and do not sit on and on at the table, but make way for others when, for you, the feast is over.

Such is the doctrine of Epicurus, as presented by Lucretius in more than seven thousand lines of superb poetry. Epicurus himself wrote three hundred books; all but three letters to pupils giving summaries of parts of his teaching, two collections of aphorisms, and some few fragments of his works have been destroyed. However, other writers, who record his career and analyze his work, tell us enough of it to make it clear that Lucretius's *Nature of the Universe* is not a flat verse transcription of the founder's theory, but a highly personal document which must be handled sensitively and imaginatively if we are to understand it.

The difference between the doctrine of Epicurus and the poem of Lucretius is far more than the difference between prose (crabbed technical Greek prose) and verse (rolling melodious Latin hexameters). It is the difference between assured serenity and repressed excitement; between cool conviction and eager persuasion; and, ultimately, between certainty and doubt. Epicurus teaches like a man who never felt a tremor in his heart or a shadow fall on his intellect. Lucretius argues with a tense urgency that ranges all the way from the exultation of a triumphal hymn, through the slangy bitterness of social satire, to the hopeless melancholy of a dirge.

And why? Whom is he trying to convince?

Lucretius dedicates *The Nature of the Universe* to a Roman nobleman called Memmius, whom he treats as a friend and a potential convert:

> *It is your merit, and the pleasure I shall reap*
> *from your sweet friendship, which persuade me to endure*
> *this toilsome effort, spending many peaceful nights*
> *in search of phrases and poetic melody*
> *to kindle a bright light within your intellect*
> *and show you all the secrets of the universe.*

Yet Memmius appears only a dozen times throughout the poem: in the first, second, and fifth books. In the last book he is not even mentioned. From a private letter of Cicero we learn that, having acquired the old house of Epicurus in Athens, Memmius proposed to tear it down and build a palace for himself on the site—although it was a shrine revered by all Epicurus's followers. Does this not mean that he remained unconverted to Epicureanism (which indeed was alien to his restless, greedy character), and that Lucretius dedicated the work to him merely as a conventional civility?

The poem seems rather to be aimed at you, the sympathetic reader. "You must have noticed," says Lucretius, and we assent; or he says, "Come, let me tell you," and we follow his argument. This is a didactic poem, then, meant not for one man but for all who wish to understand the nature of the universe.

Yet, if we read the poem carefully, not simply as a nexus of scientific theorems but as a series of emotional experiences, we shall notice something else. It is profoundly pessimistic. Epicurus's teaching is, on the whole, optimistic. Life, it holds, is easy to enjoy if you are sensible about it: a few friends, a retired garden, simple food, a tranquil mind, these are the sum of human welfare. Excitement—sexual passion, the intoxication of wine, or any emotional outburst—is highly dangerous; gloomy forebodings and dismal sights should naturally be shunned. Now consider the shape of Lucretius's poem. It opens with a magnificent, full-chorded paean to Venus, mother of the Romans, bringer of peace, personifica-

tion of pleasure, spirit of spring and love and creative Nature —a wonderful passage which inspired Botticelli to paint *Mars and Venus*. Some seven thousand lines later it ends with a detailed clinical and sociological account of the fearful epidemic of typhus which devastated Athens during the Peloponnesian War four centuries before. This description comes in logically enough. Lucretius is explaining a number of curious phenomena which seem to be incomprehensible —lightning strokes, earthquakes, volcanic eruptions—and thereby demonstrating that the atomic theory makes them all intelligible. In due time he reaches epidemics. These, he says, are caused by tiny invisible particles inimical to human and animal life, which are carried by the air and taken in through breathing, and which sometimes corrupt water, grass, and green crops. This is an intelligent anticipation of the germ theory. Lucretius might have stopped there. Instead, he goes on to turn into somber poetry the description of the plague at Athens given by the historian Thucydides. Detail after grisly detail is given, with an emotional fervor quite different from that of a historian: the throat closed by swollen ulcers, the tongue dripping with blood, the breath as foul as the stench of a decaying corpse, burning fever, insanity, interrupted breathing, at last the signs of death in the hollowed cheeks and nostrils and bared teeth. Enough? No. Lucretius does not stop there; he goes on, still with the same febrile, fascinated attention, to describe the disintegration of society, the sick dying in the streets, the many corpses lying unburied, and the sad rites of burial thus perverted.

> *Panic and hideous poverty persuaded them*
> *to run amok and seize the pyres built up by others*
> *and lay the corpses of their own kinsfolk upon them*
> *and kindle them forthwith: they came to blows and*
>   *bloodshed,*
> *fighting in fury, rather than desert the corpses.*

These are the last words. This is the end of a poem designed to free mankind from fear, to teach that life can be understood and lived out in a state of tranquil happiness.

You will at once say that this passage is unfinished; that the description has not been completed. It breaks off in the midst of a scene of demoralization, with no paragraph to round out and emphasize the initial purpose of the whole discussion: the argument that epidemic diseases, however horrible, have a logical explanation. True. Writing long afterward, Saint Jerome states that Cicero "emended" the poem. This may mean that he corrected a few faults of diction; or it may mean that he (or his brother Quintus, who also read it) actually prepared the poem for publication. If so, Lucretius died leaving it incomplete. There remains, unresolved, the hideous discord between the opening of the poem and its present close; between the Epicurean doctrine of tranquil pleasure enjoyed by individuals and this overattentive description of the physical and moral collapse of a civilization.

We find the same dissonance elsewhere. The poem is set out in six books. Each of the six opens with a grand, confident invocation, glorifying the godlike genius of Epicurus, extolling the freedom from fear given by true philosophy, and so forth. Of the six, only one closes optimistically, with a rising curve; one has a neutral and apparently imperfect conclusion; the other four end in thoughts of gloom, dissolution, and death. Book II, for instance, fades out with a picture of a despairing farmer trying to wring crops out of our aging and exhausted earth—a picture that makes an irreconcilable antithesis to Book I, with its glorification of Nature ever young and fresh. Book III, after calmly explaining that, since the soul is mortal, death is nothing to be feared, moves into this grim final chord:

> *Prolong your life for many years, for centuries;*
> *yet none the less eternal death will still be waiting,*
> *and he who ends his life before sunset today*
> *will be no more through the same vast eternity*
> *as he who perished many months or years before.*

I emphasize these structural contrasts because Roman writers paid special attention to the preludes and finales of their poems and of each main section of their poems, and because I do not believe critics have paid adequate attention to these discords in Lucretius. The last book opens with a glorification of Athens as the birthplace of agriculture and civilization and the supreme philosopher Epicurus, and breaks off in a description of the devastating plague of Athens.

On a smaller scale the same clash of major and minor keys can be heard throughout the poem. Again and again, in a passage that opens with serene confidence in Epicurean logic and the liberating power of the intellect, Lucretius will falter, and flag, and begin to brood, while the firmness of his reasoning seems to be overborne by the dark, confused power of his imagination. What begins as a clear-brained, optimistic analysis of a problem changes into something more like the cloudy, melancholy monologues of Hamlet.

And on a far larger scale there is another problem. Admitting that the last book is imperfect, and supposing that we could somehow reconstruct its lost or unwritten conclusion—would the poem then be complete? Most critics seem to fancy it would. They consider that these six books—which give us a reasonably complete Epicurean analysis of the physical universe, the body-and-soul unity, the inception of this world and the evolution of mankind, the sexual instinct, the origins of religious belief, and certain major scientific questions such as volcanic activity—were all that Lucretius intended to write; yet I think they are mistaken. The central purpose of Epicurus's teaching was not to explain atoms and earthquakes, but to teach men how to live. The motive for understanding physics and cosmology and psychophysical interaction and so forth was, says Lucretius, to escape from fear—and then to learn how to live rightly. And it was

Epicurus's highly individual ethical system that made the greatest impression on Greek and Roman thinkers. Therefore I believe that Lucretius, having explained the physical universe in his first six books, meant to go on to analyze moral and social problems in his second six books: to give us the Epicurean method of attaining and preserving happiness, to explain the true meaning of "pleasure" as a state of calm well-being, to show why the wise man will shun social duties and responsibilities, prefer the status of a resident alien, and "live in secret." These essential teachings, more than any amount of knowledge about cosmology, would really bring happiness to his readers, to Memmius (if Lucretius still remembered him), and to himself.

To himself. Is that not the key to all these problems of poetic structure and imagination?

One curious statement about Lucretius appears, not in any contemporary or near-contemporary writer, but in the Christian chronicle of Saint Jerome: that he was driven mad by a love philter administered by his wife, wrote the poem in his lucid intervals, and committed suicide. A distinguished English poet who had affinities with both Virgil and Lucretius, Alfred Tennyson, accepted this statement and converted it into a remarkable dramatic monologue called *Lucretius*—a soliloquy of great power and passion spoken by a thinker who finds himself struggling against the terrible visions of madness. We have no way of judging whether it is true or not: love philters were often used by Roman women, sometimes with dire effects. And certainly there is, both in the fourth book of Lucretius's poem and in Tennyson's re-creation of his troubled mind, an unusual, un-Roman, unphilosophical interest in sex and its aberrations. In Book IV is a passage which looks as though it had been developed from Epicurus's simple warning, "Sexual intercourse has never done anyone any good and may well have done harm," into the idea that sexual activity was either a disagreeable routine, or a dangerous form of insanity, or . . . and again Lucretius drifts inconclusively away.

If we were to read the poem without knowledge of Jerome's report, we might reach a similar, but simpler, conclusion. A poet who vacillates between lofty confidence in reason and feverish fascination with decay and death, whose arguments are often compulsively repetitive and sometimes trail away into half-comprehensible reveries, and whose final lines describe, with gruesome intensity, mania and death—was he not endeavoring, through meditation upon those doctrines which with great technical and linguistic skill he turned from hard Greek prose into rich Latin poetry, to liberate, not Memmius or his other readers, but himself, from the horror of great darkness? And did he succeed, or fail?

Dr. Highet, a frequent writer for Horizon, *is Anthon Professor of Latin at Columbia University. His latest book,* The Anatomy of Satire *(Princeton University Press, 1962), won the Award of Merit of the American Philological Association.*

OUTWARD SIGNS OF INWARD GRACE

England's law is the parent of our own, but to anyone who has studied both in action, the child often seems a foundling. Perhaps it will refresh a few of our readers who may have passed recently through the noisy, informal courts of our own country to have the following glimpse of a system of justice that is still swift, sure, and dignified—indeed, on many occasions a pageant of genuine antique charm. In the words of the late Lord Justice Birkett, "The various elements which make up the life of legal London continue to hold great fascination for lawyers; but they also have an enduring appeal to men and women everywhere who love tradition and the continuity of our way of life. For legal London is not the creation of lawyers alone; it belongs, in part, to the great creative artists, the men of imagination and insight like Dickens and Thackeray and Fielding and Charles Lamb, who have given it a kind of immortality and spread its fame through the world . . ."

By FRANCIS COWPER

Westminster Hall was the seedbed of our law. Within the very area enclosed by its walls the law of England emerged and evolved and was developed by the judges of the courts which sat in it. First raised in the eleventh century by William Rufus near the east end of Edward the Confessor's royal Abbey, it was rebuilt in the fourteenth century under Richard II, vast and spacious as we now know it, spanned by the great hammer-beam roof which was among the chief wonders of medieval craftsmanship. Only concentrated efforts saved it in the great blaze of 1834 which destroyed the rest of the Palace of Westminster, a jumble of halls and a labyrinth of passages, and afterward it was, with almost equal difficulty, saved from demolition in the overenthusiastic clearing of the site for the new Houses

Illustrated by FELIKS TOPOLSKI

Félix Topolski

Procession of the Lord Mayor departs from the Law Courts after his swearing-in

The Law Courts

of Parliament. In our own time it has survived the bombs and the flames of the Second World War.

It was soon after Magna Carta had enacted that the Court of Common Pleas should be held in some "certain place" (instead of following the king, wherever he might be) that the Court was settled in Westminster Hall near the great north door, and there, despite the bitter drafts which blew upon it in that exposed place, it sat for five hundred years, a monument of habit, tradition, and physical tenacity. In the two corners at the upper end of the Hall the courts of King's Bench and Chancery came to be settled just as immovably. For most of the time the courts were not even enclosed, save by a low barrier separating them from the body of the Hall, and against the unoccupied wall space were set counters and stalls where booksellers and law stationers sold their wares side by side with seamstresses offering

gloves and ribbons, and dealers in novelties displaying wares such as combs and pocket looking glasses in little ivory cases. Evidence was a commodity for sale too, and professional witnesses were always present in the Hall ready to swear to anything if hired by some disreputable lawyer.

Across Westminster Hall, then, has moved in the flesh the continuous and unbroken procession of the fathers of the law of England from the days of the Plantagenets to those of George IV: Gascoigne, More, Coke, Hale, Holt, Mansfield—these very walls have heard the voice of every one of them.

Nor was it only for the day-to-day and year-to-year routine of hearing and determining disputes between man and man or between the Crown and its subjects that the scene was set in Westminster Hall. Century after century its central space has formed the back-

Procession of the Lord Mayor departs from the Law Courts after his swearing-in

ground for the great dramas and tragedies and set pieces of the State trials, when the processes of law became a spectacle for the nation and for the world. Here, during a hearing of one hundred forty-five days spread over a period of seven years, Warren Hastings faced his accusers, while the whole exotic and chaotic pageant of the foundation of England's Indian Empire unfolded itself before the listeners. Here was played out the fashionable eighteenth-century farce of the trial for bigamy of the scandalously adventurous Duchess of Kingston or (as her conviction proved her to be) Countess of Bristol. Here, before a revolutionary tribunal packed with his enemies presided over by a second-rate barrister, King Charles I received sentence of death with a calmness and courage which redeemed the vacillations of his life. In this place, where he had sat as Lord Chancellor, Sir Thomas More, "the King's good servant, but God's first," was trapped and condemned by perjured evidence.

The law has deserted Westminster Hall, but it is still linked with the Palace of Westminster, for the ultimate court of appeal for England, Scotland, and Northern Ireland is still the House of Lords.

And to approach the House of Lords one may pass through Westminster Hall, which was once in a perpetual bustle of barristers, attorneys, clients, witnesses, and miscellaneous sightseers, but from which the tides of the law have so long receded. Now, where so much was passionately or acutely argued, where so much was achieved and suffered, there is only a vast emptiness as of a wide, deserted shore.

After the ancient Palace of Westminster had been destroyed in 1834, in the blaze which a contemporary writer rather stiffly described as "a *tableau vivant* of not inferior interest," a suggestion was made that a Palace of Justice should be built separately from the new Houses of Parliament to accommodate the Superior Courts of the realm.

The first idea of a site for this proposed new Palace of Justice, as suggested in a petition to Parliament in 1836, was Lincoln's Inn Fields. In 1841 a select committee of both Houses was appointed to consider the matter. However, objections to building on one of inner London's few open spaces became vocal, and in 1845 an alternative site between the Strand and Carey Street was put forward and soon gained favor. It was a picturesque but dilapidated and poverty-stricken area,

so complex with its courtyards and alleys that little boys used to earn pennies by guiding strangers through it from St. Clement Danes to Lincoln's Inn.

When the uncertainty over the site was dispelled, doubt and debate arose over the design. Eventually the plans of George Edward Street, a distinguished ecclesiastical architect, were adopted on the ground of their magnificence rather than their practicality, and he was allowed to cover the five acres at his disposal with an interesting and impressive but fantastically complex exhibition piece of ecclesiastical Gothic, to house not only the courts but also, of course, all the officials on whom the working of the machinery of the law depends. The vast Central Hall was rather like the Upper Church at Assisi (without the Giottos). It was paved with mosaics which have ever since been constantly under repair. The courtrooms off narrow corridors on the floor above somewhat resembled the side chapels of a cathedral. The drinking bar, for the refreshment of lawyers and litigants, irresistibly recalled a monastic crypt. The Bar Library (an afterthought) was isolated aloft very near the top of the building. The State opening by Queen Victoria in January, 1883, was an occasion of great pageantry and magnificence.

The Law Courts have changed relatively little since 1883. The former drinking crypt has been lately transformed into a restaurant. Slick paint work and modern lighting, according ill with the massive pillars, have dispelled the dim, religious, and rather impressive shades of former times. During the Second World War one of the Chancery Courts was hit by a medium-sized bomb, and the deep scars of the explosion still pit the stonework of the corridor outside. The present Probate, Divorce, and Admiralty wing, added in 1911, was more heavily damaged and is still only partly repaired. About the time of the First World War some rather flimsy hutments were erected as temporary courts in one of the quadrangles. They are still there and in the passage of years have almost acquired the status of historic interest.

Foreigners passing down the Strand commonly mistake the building for a church. It has been called "the grave of modern Gothic," and as such it is a fine and spacious mausoleum twice as interesting in its complex arrangement as the Hampton Court maze and full of genuinely fine Victorian craftsmanship in stone. In almost eighty years the legal profession has got used to working there.

A Solicitor's Office in Gray's Inn

Barristers and Solicitors

Barristers work in chambers; solicitors work in offices. The nonlegal citizen usually imagines that this is a "snob" distinction without a difference. It is not. The distinction is functional. Solicitors are in a sense legal businessmen and normally employ the same sort of staff as businessmen do—clerks of all grades, secretaries, typists, office boys, receptionists, cashiers, switchboard girls. Not so the members of the Bar.

While the barrister is the consultant of the legal world, practicing the arts of forensic surgery in the operating theatres of the courts, the solicitor is the general practitioner of the law, not only prescribing for his clients in a crisis but also maintaining their legal health as their day-to-day adviser. Of course in England, where everything has grown organically and nothing has been coherently planned, no distinction is quite so simple as that; but, generally speaking, the solicitor is an office

man. Whoever is in doubt on the legal implications of his situation, or on the legal consequences of his acts or of somebody else's acts in relation to him, does well to consult a good solicitor.

All the barristers in London are grouped in the Temple and Lincoln's Inn on the doorstep of the Law Courts; solicitors are everywhere—in the traditional precincts of the Inns of Court, amid the solid commercial assurance of the city, in the rather showier offices of the West End, in shopping centers in the outer suburbs. A few work alone, most work in partnership; some firms have a dozen partners. There are homely firms with a personal touch. There are firms so large, so streamlined, so compartmented, that they are virtually law factories; your problem goes into one end of the machinery as raw material and comes out at the other end tied up in a neat bundle and solved. There are

stately firms, old established against a mercantile background, who would turn up their noses at anything but the heaviest of commercial cases. There are fashionable firms who deal in scandals and divorces in high places at home and abroad and in almost every one of whose cupboards skeletons rattle. There are old-fashioned family solicitors who keep the great families from ruin at the hands of the Chancellor of the Exchequer by an intimate and curious knowledge of the loopholes in taxation. Rarely does Mr. Jaggers of *Great Expectations* have his counterparts in the vicinity of the criminal courts, tough, disillusioned men whose practice has taught them as much about crime as their clients know. In these busy days, firms like Dodson and Fogg in *Pickwick Papers* are nearly extinct, firms which will make a mountain of litigation out of a molehill of a dispute.

The barrister works as an individualist in a co-operative setting, never in partnership. His services are essentially personal. It is his opinion, his learning, his persuasiveness in advocacy, that he puts at the disposal of his clients. He is an artist in law. He might well write over his doorpost: "All my own work."

It is not so long since the barrister was a complete individualist. A hundred years ago a man took a set of chambers in one of the Inns of Court and waited in heartbreaking solitude for solicitors to bring him work. Thence he would sally forth to travel from assize to assize, to go to sessions, to haunt the Old Bailey, or to attend the courts daily in Westminster Hall, hoping to pick up a few crumbs of reputation by helping overbusy seniors. As a young bachelor he usually made his practicing chambers his home. Apart from his laundress (the Inns of Court term for a charwoman), a small scruffy boy might be his only attendant, part office boy, part "boots." This free and easy, unconventional, essentially masculine way of life in chambers was vividly depicted by Thackeray in *Pendennis*. It was not regarded as correct for a married man to live with his wife and family in his practicing chambers. A female domestic influence would have transformed the atmosphere.

Even rich and successful leaders of the Bar dispensed with conventional amenities in their practicing chambers. Remember Mr. Serjeant Snubbin's room as described by Dickens in *Pickwick Papers*: "Books of practice, heaps of papers, and opened letters, were scattered over the table, without any attempt at order or arrangement; the furniture of the room was old and rickety; the doors of the bookcase were rotting in their hinges; the dust flew out from the carpet in little clouds at every step; the blinds were yellow with age and dirt;

the state of everything in the room showed, with a clearness not to be mistaken, that Mr. Serjeant Snubbin was far too much occupied with his professional pursuits to take any great heed or regard of his personal comforts."

An established barrister, then, would be attended by a single clerk and already that clerk had assumed the character which he largely retains today, that of a servant in name, but in a relationship rather like that of Mr. Pickwick and Sam Weller or Don Quixote and Sancho Panza: there was nothing servile about his services.

Gradually the institution of one-man chambers vanished. The increasing number of men at the Bar, the transmigration of the judges in the 1880's from Westminster and Lincoln's Inn to the now centralized Law Courts in the Strand—these and other changing circumstances produced the system now established. A senior barrister will rent a set of chambers from his Inn of Court and will sublet rooms or shares of rooms to other men, perhaps a dozen of them. They work in close association, but they are not partners and each has his own clients and his own individual fee book. In some chambers there will be a high degree of specialization—Admiralty, patents, taxation, heavy commercial cases—but in most Temple chambers the work is mixed—Common Law work on the civil side, contracts and torts, landlord and tenant, criminal law, divorce. In the chambers in Lincoln's Inn the Chancery men congregate to deal with conveyances of land, trusts and settlements, interpretation of wills, custody of infants.

Many of the chambers in the Inns of Court (including some among the most prosperous and the best frequented) have an air of Dickensian antiquity—a combination of mustiness, dustiness, and the charm of old, pleasantly proportioned rooms. Side by side with these there have arisen in the rebuilding after the bombardments of the Second World War a crop of lighter, brighter, smarter, showier, parquet-floored, pseudo-Georgian buildings, very clean and mostly quite without any character at all.

As recently as the early 1920's there was a leader of the Admiralty Bar who gave "pupils' parties" in King's Bench Walk. At the climax of the celebration everyone stood on the tables and a bag of rats was emptied out to be hunted through the chambers by a couple of terriers. About the same time an enthusiastic yachtsman, one of the last exponents of the one-man chambers system, built a dinghy in the entrance hall of his chambers in old Crown Office Row and launched it at the Temple Stairs. You see the psychological difference between "office" and "chambers."

The Judges of England

If you happened to be passing Westminster Abbey one morning early in October you would hear the air filled with the pealing of all the bells. And below, by the great west door and in Dean's Yard and the Cloisters, you would see a bustle of arrival and preparation as judges emerged from their motorcars in scarlet and ermine, and Queen's Counsel in black knee breeches, black silk stockings, buckled shoes, black silk gowns, lace jabots, and great wigs decorated the scene, for all the world like gentlemen out of an eighteenth-century play. This is the start of the ceremonials which mark the end of the Long Vacation and the beginning of the legal year, a special service to which the Lord Chancellor in his heavy robes of black and gold leads the judges of England and the Bar of England in a corporate act of worship.

Immediately after the Abbey service, which may be regarded as a prolonged grace to the Lord Chancellor's breakfast, the judges and the more distinguished members of the Bar are received by him in the Royal Gallery at the House of Lords and entertained to a standing collation. It is in the crossing from the east end of the Abbey to the Houses of Parliament that the glory and pageantry of the law are displayed to the Londoner in the street. First comes the Lord Chancellor, preceded by his great gilt mace and the heavy square purse of the Great Seal, tasselled and richly embroidered with the Royal Arms. Each is borne by an officer in the knee breeches, buckled shoes, and lace jabot of Court dress. Behind the Lord Chancellor walk his trainbearer and another officer. Then come the judges in file: first the Lord Chief Justice in scarlet and ermine, wearing the golden chain which is the badge of his office, a heavy collar of double SS interlaced, that has been a badge of honor since the days of the House of Lancaster. Next, the Master of the

Rolls, the President of the Probate, Divorce, and Admiralty Division, and the Lords Justices of the Court of Appeal, in heavy black and gold robes similar to those of the Lord Chancellor. After them come the Justices of the High Court, all in scarlet and ermine; then the Queen's Counsel; then the junior counsel.

Another legal year has begun, and for the day-to-day business the lawyers discard their "review order" for their "service dress." Knee breeches and buckled shoes are laid by. The lace jabot is replaced by plain white linen bands. This is one of the rare occasions when the judges and Queen's Counsel wear their "full-bottomed" wigs, the great wigs approximating those of the period of Queen Anne. For normal court wear they have the smaller-tailed wigs developed from the "tiewigs" of the later eighteenth century.

Why do lawyers wear wigs? To answer by origins, it is because in the long-haired epoch of the early seven-

teenth century Louis XIII of France went bald at thirty and started the fashion of the flowing wig. The return of the exiled English Royalists after the Cromwellian interlude brought the mode to England, but until the end of the century the elderly and old-fashioned still wore their own hair. In the eighteenth century the lawyers followed the general habit of dress at the time, and in the nineteenth century, when wigs went out, they never lost the habit. They have simply perpetuated a frozen fashion.

Why robes at all? From a purely practical point of view, they are great levelers, so far as the Bar is concerned. In robes the most poverty-stricken junior will not be put out of countenance by any man in court and will not be at any disadvantage in the face of the opulent confidence of a Savile Row suit on a fashionable opponent. The uniform is also a permanent reminder of professional discipline, not a guarantee of good behavior, but a great aid to it. As for the judges, we can agree with the most extreme of the so-called "utilitarians" that a judge sitting naked on a packing case would have just as much law in his head, just as much strength in his personality, as if he wore the most resplendent robes. But in human affairs it has always been found practical to have outward signs of inward grace, in higher affairs just as much as in the case of the barber's pole or the inn's signboard. It is only when the inward grace is absent that one need start complaining. Robes and uniforms are not so much symbols as a language of their own. The robes of the judges, part medieval, part Tudor, part Stuart, part eighteenth-century, speak of a continuity of development of responsibility. They clothe the individual with the corporate authority of the law. They remind him that he is not an isolated individual acting for himself alone, here today and gone tomorrow; that his task is not a mere matter of whim or fancy, but is one which, in the light of history, is weighty with the centuries and as splendid as scarlet and gold.

The flexible, loosely defined English way of selecting judges from among practicing barristers suits England well. It works by patronage from aloft, exercised, however, with a due, if unexpressed, regard for the general opinion of a profession which assesses its members very shrewdly for their integrity, their strength of character, their learning, and their experience of the Courts; and, after appointment, a judge's security of tenure is, for all practical purposes, indefeasible. There are, of course, imperfections in all human affairs. Accidents in appointments will happen now and then. Politics have been known at times to thrust upon the Bench a quota of persons "of tried incompetence." But, over the centuries, the judges of England, as an institution in society, have maintained a prestige and commanded a respect that can only be a reflection of their quality in the function entrusted to them.

The judges stand not only for justice as between citizen and citizen but, in our own day as in many preceding ages, more important still, as a rampart for the individual human person against the pressure, which would otherwise be overwhelming, of the power of the organized State, ever pushing toward a condition of society subordinated to its despotic will.

The English legal world, as so many other English institutions, is like an old house which has been altered, adapted, extended, refurnished across the generations, sometimes for convenience, sometimes for necessity, sometimes even for fun, but which has never been pulled down and rebuilt from the foundations. No Justinian, no Napoleon, has ever made *tabula rasa* of all that has gone before to start afresh with a code of his own devising. So in the rambling old house of English law there are tortuous passages, dark corners, even some accumulations of antiquated rubbish, but there are also splendid lofty halls full of light and air and majesty. It is a house that is lived in, and the Englishman feels that it is his home, for it fits the way of life to which he is accustomed, a way of life that is easy-fitting and not too rigid. If there is some junk in the attic, there is good wine in the cellars; there are many fine portraits on the walls, and the windows look out on a wide landscape of ancient freedom, even though there have been times when those windows needed cleaning and polishing afresh. England has never made the mistake of trying to create for itself an "ideal" law. For it there has been

No abstract intellectual plan of life
Quite irrespective of life's plainest laws,
But one, a man, who is a man and nothing more,
May lead within a world which (by your leave)
Is Rome or London—not Fool's—paradise.

And that man is the free and lawful man, imperfect and limited, but made by the Creator in his own image, about whom the Common Law of England has grown with all the flexibility of a living thing.

In that spirit, the Bench and Bar of England are not legal technicians, but men whose professional training has merged with its obligations to eat and drink together and become absorbed into the spirit and the public opinion of their profession, making themselves one with what has gone before and what shall come after. The old sundial high on the wall of Pump Court in the Temple reminds each passing generation: "Shadows we are and like shadows depart." But the law remains and lives because it has caught a reflection of the eternal.

Feliks Topolski is the ebullient Polish-born artist who, for the past twenty-five years or so, has been recording his impressions of the passing scene in London and elsewhere (see his Coronation murals in HORIZON *for November, 1960). Francis Cowper is the official law reporter in the House of Lords. This article was adapted from* Topolski's Legal London, *published by Stevens and Sons Limited.*

"I have
discovered
that

our great favourite, Miss Austen,

is my country-woman. . . .
with whom mamma before her marriage
was acquainted. Mamma says
that she was then the prettiest,
silliest, most affected,
husband-hunting butterfly she ever remembers."

—MARY RUSSELL MITFORD, 1815*

A 1964 appraisal
by J. CHRISTOPHER HEROLD

That Jane Austen's life was singularly uneventful is a cliché as dear to her admirers as to her detractors. But what is meant by uneventful? It is true that she never lost her virginity, never met a celebrity, never traveled farther from her native Hampshire than Lyme Regis, Bath, and London, never left the genteel circle of upper middle-class society (though she had a few glimpses into the world of fashion and the world of squalor), never sought nor enjoyed publicity, and never underwent a spiritual crisis or experienced anything in the least bit sensational. Except for the hours she stole for her writing, the forty-two years of her life were devoted to her family; and it was not until her thirty-sixth year that her writing gained a wider audience than her family circle. Her first three published novels—*Sense and Sensibility, Pride and Prejudice,* and *Mansfield Park*—appeared anonymously; only in 1816, the year before her death, did her name become known to the public. She died a professional aunt rather than a professional author. Her total earnings from the four novels published in her lifetime amounted to less than £1000, and even the warmest admirers of these novels could find no higher praise than to esteem them worthy of being placed next to the works of Fanny Burney and of Maria Edgeworth.

The most noteworthy incidents impinging on Jane's existence were either undramatic or peripheral: her cousin Eliza, Comtesse de Feuillide, lost her husband to the guillotine in the Reign of Terror. Her aunt, Mrs. Leigh Perrot, was ludicrously arrested for shoplifting in

*Mary Russell Mitford, an English novelist and dramatist, is not related to Jessica, Nancy, and Unity except by virtue of her sharp tongue.

Illustrated with frontispieces from the 1833 editions of Miss Austen's novels

SENSE AND SENSIBILITY

Lucy shows Elinor a locket "proving" her betrothal to Edward. But the lie does not shake sensible Elinor, who triumphs later when she *marries Edward.*

Bath, risked a death sentence, since the amount involved exceeded five shillings, and spent several miserable months as a prisoner in the lodgings of the jailer of Ilchester before being acquitted. Her brother Henry, turned banker after an abortive military career, went bankrupt but cheerfully transcended that disaster by taking holy orders and entering the ministry. Another brother, Edward, who had been adopted by a childless landowner named Knight, lost part of his very large inheritance to some of Mr. Knight's relatives when they sued him. Her brother Francis, captain of H.M.S. *Canopus,* almost took part in the Battle of Trafalgar but missed it by a few hours. Jane herself was almost engaged to one young man, whom she appears to have loved very much but who died before the engagement became formal, and was actually engaged for half a day to another young man, until her doubts as to whether she really loved him made her break off the engagement and fly to Bath—the only impulsive action in her life.

To those who regard experience as a necessary prerequisite for the unfolding of genius, Jane Austen must appear as hopelessly handicapped. To some of her contemporaries—and to a number of her critics ever since—her novels appeared to be "mean": all they deal with is young girls trying to get married and, by some improbable denouement, attaining their goal despite themselves; no hero or heroine is ever introduced without a precise state-

ment of his or her annual income and future expectations. Violent passions are absent from her world. The most catastrophic incidents in her novels are Marianne Dashwood's attack of influenza *(Sense and Sensibility)* and Louisa's fall down the stone steps at Lyme Regis *(Persuasion).* In her novels as well as in her letters any demonstrative form of enthusiasm for music and poetry, any symptom of religious zeal or metaphysical uneasiness —in short, any romantic notion—is treated as an utterly suspect pretension. In her hatred (perhaps also fear?) of sentimentality in any form, Jane Austen bordered on Philistinism at one extreme and on cynicism at the other. Equally striking is the virtual absence of references to the world-shaking events and developments of her day—not only in her fiction but also in her letters. The French Revolution is never alluded to anywhere. The rise of industrialism seems to have escaped her notice. The reawakening of religious conscience that characterized her age finds no echo whatever in her fiction.

The period of Jane Austen's creative activity was also the era of the Napoleonic wars, of England's struggle for national survival. With two of her brothers serving in the Navy (both of them later attained Admiral's rank), one might suppose that she would not ignore these events completely. Nor did she; yet only a few allusions to military events stand out in her work. In *Persuasion,* for example, she at last comes to grips with the Napoleonic wars. The time is 1814; Sir Walter Elliot of Kellynch Hall, having squandered a great deal of money, is obliged to consider letting his ancestral home; his solicitor is on hand one morning following the conclusion of peace (after twenty-two years of war). Laying down his newspaper, the solicitor says: "I must take leave to observe, Sir Walter, that the present juncture is much in our favor. This peace will be turning all our rich naval officers ashore. They will be all wanting a home. Could not be a better time, Sir Walter, for having a choice of tenants, very responsible tenants. Many a noble fortune has been made during the war." It is submitted that nowhere in literature have the blessings of peace been understated more emphatically.

There is no denying that the outward events of Jane Austen's life were of no moment except to herself and to her family. Nor does her inner life appear to have been very rich except as it related to her creative genius. If she had a passion, it was an uncompromising love of truth and an unforgiving horror of sentimentality and pretense—a horror so extreme that she suspected as fraudulent in others emotions that she could not feel herself. She knew love, no doubt—but it was the love of a spirited young woman with a strong sense of decorum and without sexual experience. Characteristically, the lovers in her novels never kiss or even hold hands, and the men with whom her heroines fall in love have something mysterious and inscrutable about them: a man's world was closed territory to her. Not that she was a prude or ignorant of the facts of life. The heroes and heroines of her earliest productions, written when she was fourteen or fifteen, are alarmingly addicted to love out of wedlock and to grand larceny. But these productions are pure parody and buffoonery. In her mature work illicit or adulterous love does occur on several occasions, it is true: in *Sense and Sensibility* Mr. Willoughby begets an illegitimate child by a young woman who is herself illegitimate; in *Pride and Prejudice* Lydia briefly lives in sin with Mr. Wickham (who, incidentally, is also guilty of financial indelicacy—the most serious nonsexual crime in any of Jane Austen's mature novels); in *Mansfield Park* Admiral Crawford lives with a mistress and Mr. Crawford abducts, or rather is abducted by, Mrs. Rushworth, whom her husband divorces; in *Persuasion* the scheming Mrs. Clay is set up in London by the duplicitous Sir William Elliot, who, in punishment for his sins, will be "wheedled and caressed at last into making her [his] wife."

None of these scandalous events, however, is described in detail; the reader hears of them only as he would hear gossip—either from the mouths of other characters or, in a succinct statement, from the author. Where her intuitive knowledge is complete, Jane Austen re-creates the minutest shadings of emotion in their totality, but where it is wanting, she is content to represent events and actions not in themselves but indirectly, as they strike the consciousness of characters not immediately involved.

That Jane Austen could describe what a woman feels when she loves must be clear to anyone who has read *Persuasion,* the last novel she completed. What she expresses here is a triumphant satisfaction arising not so much from physical passion as from moral certainty and peace. The title of the novel is deliberately ambiguous: eight years before the action of the novel begins, its heroine, Anne Elliot, had been *persuaded* by an elder friend that the man to whom she was engaged—Captain Wentworth of the Royal Navy—was not the man for her; being in doubt of her feelings, she had canceled the engagement—for, as Jane Austen wrote to her niece Fanny Knight, "Anything is to be preferred or endured rather than marrying without Affection." At the end of the novel, Anne is *persuaded* not only of her continued love for Wentworth but also of his for her. She has just received his written declaration of love when they meet accidentally in the streets of Bath and he offers to escort her home. Anne accepts the offer, and, "smiles reined in and spirits dancing in private rapture," they proceed on their walk:

There they exchanged again those feelings and those promises which had once before seemed to secure everything, but which had been followed by so many, many years of division and estrangement. There they had

PRIDE AND PREJUDICE

Mr. Bennet agrees to Elizabeth's marriage when she reveals that her fiancé secretly provided her sister's dowry and thus saved the Bennets from disgrace.

returned again into the past, more exquisitely happy, perhaps in their reunion, than when it had been first projected; more tender, more tried, more fixed in a knowledge of each other's character, truth, and attachment; more equal to act, more justified in acting. And there, as they slowly paced the gradual ascent, heedless of every group around them, seeing neither sauntering politicians, bustling housekeepers, flirting girls, nor nursery maids and children, they could indulge in those retrospections and acknowledgements, and especially in those explanations of what had directly preceded the present moment, which were so poignant and so ceaseless in interest. All the little variations of the last week were gone through; and of yesterday and today there could scarcely be an end.

Jane Austen's fortunately rare attempts at verse prove a decided lack of talent for poetry; yet here, in these few lyrical, soaring lines, she expresses all the ecstasy of certainty in love. The reader whose eyes follow that pair of "spirits dancing in private rapture" cannot help but be persuaded, or at least hope, that their marriage will be a happy one indeed, and that all their tomorrows will be but a prolongation of today.

Although the mating of couples in lawful wedlock is the stuff on which all Jane Austen's novels feed, it is only in her last book, when her life's strength was ebbing away and she was dying of cancer, that she allowed herself to release such lyricism. In her earlier books there are no comparable passages: the reader is

MANSFIELD PARK

"When I wear this necklace," Fanny exuded in her best orphan thankfulness as she accepted Mary's gift, "I will always . . . feel how very kind you were."

somehow miraculously made aware that the heroine is in love by innumerable indirect and minute hints whose significance grows on him almost as gradually as on the heroine herself. It may be objected that love between the sexes is not the only form of love; that there are other forms with which Jane Austen must have been more familiar. Her entire life was spent with what seems to have been an exceptionally lovable and affectionate family. It is surprising, then, that in her novels pictures of family happiness are far rarer than the opposite: her characters' affections for their relatives are highly selective. The friendship between Jane and Elizabeth Bennet in *Pride and Prejudice* is as perfect as was that between Jane Austen and her sister Cassandra, but in the novel the two friends feel far from tender toward their younger sisters; Fanny Price, in *Mansfield Park,* is devoted to her dashing sailor brother William but regards her mother as a slattern and is ashamed of her father. As for Jane Austen's attitude toward children, it has often been said that she disliked them. This accusation, based on a few quotations out of context, is extremely unfair, even though it is hardly a crime to dislike children. What Jane makes amply clear is that she dislikes *some* children and *all* doting parents. But perhaps even more relevant to her psychology is her aversion to what she called "mothering"—that is, childbearing.

There can be no question that even though Jane Austen re-

garded married love as the greatest bliss on earth, she was aware that the price to be paid for it often exceeded the bliss itself. Families were large in those days, especially the families of clergymen (being poor, she could hardly expect to marry anybody but a clergyman), and deaths from childbirth were common. To judge the effects of excessive "mothering," she had but to observe her nearest acquaintances, her sisters-in-law, her nieces. To her niece Fanny Knight she wrote: "Do not be in a hurry [to marry]. . . . by not beginning the business of Mothering quite so early in life, you will be young in Constitution, spirits, figure, & countenance . . ." Even without mothering, Jane, who as a young woman was able to dance twenty dances at one ball without fatigue and still wish for more, was physically exhausted after twenty years of trying to take care of nieces and nephews while composing her books. Perhaps the burden of virginity seemed light to her compared to those of motherhood and conjugal duties. She was a tall, handsome girl, high-spirited, and altogether desirable as a wife. And the fact that she was poor, or that one of her suitors died, cannot account quite satisfactorily for her never marrying, especially since the horrors of the life of a penniless spinster were constantly present in her mind. No doubt if a man whom she could have loved truly and deeply had asked her to marry, she might have assumed the risks of mothering; but, without that, the advantages of being single and free at least to write books rather than cater to an indifferent husband and raise a brood of noisy children, outweighed any others.

It is a fallacy to believe that the mere accumulation of experience necessarily contributes to the development of a creative imagination. What matters is not how much experience a novelist has had but what he makes of it. The question has been asked at the beginning of this essay: What is meant by an uneventful life? To those who have eyes and wit and understanding, the most trivial happenings can be events, while it is possible for others to spend their lives in the turmoil of great passions and high adventure without ever really being aware of anything in the world save themselves. Jane Austen, who was gifted with uncommonly observant eyes as well as enviable provisions of wit and understanding, never wrote a line about herself. None of her characters, be they principals or secondary figures, can be identified with any actual person. The elements of resemblance between her fictional characters and the real ones she knew (including herself) are sometimes striking, to be sure, but they are mere elements, and the characters are genuine creations with lives of their own. To achieve this transmutation of the drab raw material that everyday life offered her into the sparkling human comedy that is the essence of her work requires more than wit and genius: it demands a peculiar blending of humility and ruthlessness. The humility is that needed to observe the unlimited variety of signs and symptoms by which even a minute and, to most observers, uninteresting sampling of humanity reveals the secret workings of mind and heart; the ruthlessness is that needed to rescue understanding from the pitfalls of maudlin sympathy. Jane Austen is as severe to her heroes as she is just to her unsympathetic characters. Mr. Bennet, one of the most lovable creations in all fiction, is nonetheless shown up in *Pride and Prejudice* as the irresponsible egotist that he is; and Mrs. Norris, the most detestable person in all of Jane Austen's cast of characters, almost moves the reader to sympathy in the last pages of *Mansfield Park,* for her infuriating conduct is shown to be motivated by a pathetic yearning to be needed.

Jane Austen's passion was for truth, and truth to her was comedy. This, of course, is a serious limitation: truth is not always amusing. Yet her few attempts to deal with more somber themes (as in *Lady Susan* and the unfinished novel, *The Watsons*) prove the wisdom of her self-imposed limitation. What she may be criticized for is not so much her decision to stick to comedy as her resolute determination to misunderstand the nature of tragedy, which she viewed either as a pose, comical in itself, or as the just reward for having strayed from the proper paths prescribed by "religious principles" and social decorum. No one would have agreed more heartily than Jane Austen herself to the proposition that her novels are in some respects much thinner and more brittle fare than many a less perfect and more pretentious work of fiction.

Virtually the entire body of Jane Austen's work is comedy, yet there is a great deal of variation in it. She began with pure—and unsurpassable—farce: *Love and Freindship.* (She wrote this as a young girl, but she spelled "freindship," and "beleive" and "adeiu" that way to the end of her life.) Another of her *juvenilia, Lesley Castle,* contains some of the most hilarious inspirations in all comic literature. In *Sense and Sensibility* the Don Quixote-Sancho Panza theme, which appears in a singularly burlesque disguise in *Lesley Castle,* is transformed into a high-comedy contrast between the excessively sober and sensible Elinor and her determinedly romantic sister, Marianne. In *Pride and Prejudice* parody is abandoned altogether and English social comedy is born, but literary parody continues, a little heavily for Jane Austen, in *Northanger Abbey,* in which the dreary charms of Gothic ruins and thrills of horror made popular by Mrs. Radcliffe are given much the same treatment that Molière gave the bluestockings and the *précieuses* of his time.

With *Mansfield Park* Jane Austen took a new direction, away from satire and epigrams and toward a more mellow and subtle form of comedy. In one of her letters she announced somewhat surprisingly that the subject of her book in progress was ordina-

A Jane Austen Sampler

From Miss Austen's LETTERS:

We have been very gay since I wrote last; dining at Nackington, returning by Moonlight, and everything quite in Stile, not to mention Mr. Claringbould's Funeral which we saw go by on Sunday.

. . . Dr. Gardiner was married yesterday to Mrs. Percy and her three daughters. . . .

I do not want people to be very agreeable, as it saves me the trouble of liking them a great deal.

From SENSE AND SENSIBILITY:

There was a kind of cold-hearted selfishness on both sides, which mutually attracted them. . .

. . . they were neither of them quite enough in love to think that three hundred and fifty pounds a year would supply them with the comforts of life.

From PRIDE AND PREJUDICE:

Miss Bingley's congratulations to her brother, on his approaching marriage, were all that was affectionate and insincere.

. . . I have often observed that resignation is never so perfect as when the blessing denied begins to lose somewhat of its value in our estimation.

From MANSFIELD PARK:

. . . there is not one in a hundred of either sex, who is not taken in when they marry. . . . it is, of all transactions, the one in which people expect most from others, and are least honest themselves."

From EMMA:

While he spoke, Emma's mind was most busy, and, with all the wonderful velocity of thought, had been able—and yet without losing a word—to catch and comprehend the exact truth of the whole; to see that Harriet's hopes had been entirely groundless . . . that Harriet was nothing; that she was every thing herself. . . . She felt for Harriet, with pain and with contrition; but no flight of generosity run mad, opposing all that could be probable or reasonable, entered her brain. . . . Her way was clear, though not quite smooth.—She spoke then, on being so entreated.—What did she say?—Just what she ought, of course. A lady always does.—She said enough to show there need not be despair—and to invite him to say more himself.

EMMA

Emma attempts to make a match between Harriet Smith, left, and Mr. Elton, looking on. Little does she know that Elton looks on her more than on Harriet.

the moral integrity of the English character, while Mary and Henry Crawford represent the cold and corrosive cynicism of the London smart set. Mansfield Park itself, in which nearly all the action takes place (except for the descent into Hell that is Fanny's trip to Portsmouth) stands quite explicitly for all that is dignified, civilized, and traditional in England. The subject of *Mansfield Park* is not merely ordination but the meaning of religion in the English social fabric. (It is the kind of religion in which it would be regarded as bad form to mention God outside a sermon or an oath, and in which the truth of "religious principles" is demonstrable chiefly by their influence on proper social conduct—a formula that has worked out remarkably well in England.)

To explain the novel in such terms tends to make it appear to be an allegory, which a novel should never be. It is nothing of the sort: Jane Austen's tour de force consists in never even suggesting that an allegory might be intended. The actors act out of the given necessities of their characters and their situations; the abstractions they might embody are never even hinted at; the mood is one of subdued comedy. (The deplorably moralizing last chapter is out of keeping with the rest of the book.)

In *Emma* Jane Austen did not attempt so complex a theme; it is a high comedy of character and probably her supreme achievement in that vein. *Persuasion* is the least sparkling of her books: apart from Sir Walter Elliot, who is a caricature, it contains no truly comic figure. Yet it glows more warmly than any of her other novels, and there is a touch of subdued romanticism in it.

Only Jane Austen devotees are likely to have read all her novels, but there is hardly anybody who has not read *Pride and Prejudice*. It is unquestionably the most entertaining of her mature books. There had never been anything like it before, nor have its innumerable imitators been able to come anywhere near its level. Its popularity rests undoubtedly on the brilliance of its characterizations, the ebullience of its wit, the universal humanity of its psychology, the nimble elegance of its style, and the irresistible comedy of its dialogue and plot. Of the heroine, Elizabeth Bennet, her creator wrote: "I must confess that I think her as delightful a creature as ever appeared in print," and one cannot but agree with her. Nor can one disagree with one of Jane Austen's biographers (Elizabeth Jenkins) when she acclaims Mr. Bennet as "one of the most remarkable figures in the whole range of English comedy" and salutes the creation of "the character of a genuinely witty man" as a unique feat. Mr. Bennet's aesthetic delight in the pompous foolishness and clumsy scheming of the sanctimoniously sycophantic Mr. Collins will forever be shared by all readers. Although every actor in the comedy is brilliantly characterized, Jane Austen surpassed herself in the terse delinea-

tion. At first glance the calling to the priesthood seems an unpromising subject for comedy, nor is it likely that many of her readers are aware that ordination *is* the central theme of the book. Yet closer examination reveals that this is indeed the subject and that Jane met her challenge brilliantly. Fanny Price, the Bertrams' adopted poor relation, embodies Christian humility, love, and patience. Edmund Bertram, her cousin and protector, being both an English gentleman and a Christian, cannot escape the conflict inherent in these qualities and remains fascinated by the cynical, elegant Mary Crawford until his eyes are opened to her shallowness and to Fanny's love—which constitutes his true consecration as a priest. Henry Crawford, the only demonic character in Jane Austen's fiction, might be a fugitive from Choderlos de Laclos's *Liaisons dangereuses;* yet even the compulsive Don Juanism that makes him, at first, desire Fanny as a novel subject for seduction, eventually succumbs to her gentle sweetness. Fanny's aunts, Lady Bertram and Mrs. Norris, are mitigated embodiments of the cardinal sins of Sloth and Envy. Sir Thomas Bertram, master of Mansfield Park, combining gentleness and justice with a rather stiff and forbidding dignity, is respected by some of the members of the cast as their judge and conscience and feared by others as a wet blanket. He is a father figure, and if it were not for the fact that he, too, has his small faults, he would be a godlike figure. As it is, he seems to embody

tion of young Mary, the intellectual in the Bennet family: "They found Mary, as usual, deep in the study of thorough bass and human nature."

Reading *Pride and Prejudice* is like drinking a bottle of champagne. "Elizabeth loved absurdities," says Jane Austen, and *Pride and Prejudice* brims over with such an abundance of bubbling absurdities that the happy reader, with his nostrils tingling and his mind befogged, is likely to mistake it for a mere comedy of manners and to fall in love with all the characters indiscriminately. Jane Austen's novels are amusing enough if read on the surface, but they yield a richer reward if reread thoughtfully. The inhabitants of Meryton and its environs, each with his endearing weakness, are by no means uniformly lovable. Most of them are excruciating bores (it is Jane Austen's unique talent to make bores entertaining); in addition Mr. Bennet is a weakling; Mrs. Bennet is not only a disastrous fool who threatens the happiness of her family, she also has the ideals of a brothel keeper; the younger Bennet sisters, in separate ways, are silly geese; Charlotte Lucas is a girl who sells her soul for security; Mr. Collins, whom Charlotte marries, is a man with the soul of a lackey and the potentialities of a tyrant; Mr. Wickham, by no means the worst of the lot, is a bounder; Mr. Bingley, with his excellent disposition, is a character remarkable for the fact that he has no character at all; Lady Catherine de Bourgh, who likes "to scold [her tenants] into harmony and plenty," is Arrogance personified. Of the truly sympathetic characters, Jane Bennet is *too* good—a fault deliberately intended by the author: she finds excuses for everybody, and her sister Elizabeth tells her, "You shall not, for the sake of one individual, change the meaning of principle and integrity." Only two among the leading characters possess the qualities of principle and integrity: Elizabeth herself and Mr. Darcy. And because they possess them and are not, like the others, static and unchangeable they are ultimately able to transcend their respective faults—Mr. Darcy his aristocratic pride, Elizabeth her middle-class prejudice against the aristocracy. There is only one other character in the book who is truly respectable—Elizabeth Bennet's uncle, Mr. Gardiner, who plies some "low" trade in the City (like Jane Austen's brother, the banker Henry Austen) and who, to his niece's great surprise, wins the unqualified esteem and friendship of the haughty Mr. Darcy.

The theme of *Pride and Prejudice* is one that has exerted a peculiar fascination over British minds for almost two centuries; it is, of course, class—not the class struggle in the crude, Marxist sense but in the sense of those subtle barriers whose existence or nonexistence seems to be the inevitably recurring topic of conversation in certain strata of English society. The Bennet family are landed gentry, although they are connected through Mrs.

NORTHANGER ABBEY

"How came I up that staircase?" Mr. Tilney replied to the terrified Catherine. "Because it is the nearest way from the stable-yard to my own chamber."

Bennet with tradespeople, lawyers, and the like; the fact that their estate is entailed threatens the family's social status—an issue viewed philosophically by the scholarly and genteel Mr. Bennet but not so by his essentially vulgar wife, whose rather weak mind is quite incapable of grappling with the concept of an entail. Mrs. Bennet's frantic and unscrupulous efforts to marry off her daughters come very near to ruining their chances of making a good marriage. On this ironical situation much of Jane Austen's comedy rests—yet were it not for the happy ending, the irony would seem more tragic than comic, and so it seems to Elizabeth Bennet, most of whose family appears to her as a curse. Only a victory over pride and prejudice can break down the social barriers between the equally aristocratic souls of Elizabeth and Mr. Darcy, and this victory they achieve despite the foolishness of the plebeian Mrs. Bennet and of the noble Lady Catherine de Bourgh.

When, in 1816, the Prince Regent's librarian suggested to Jane Austen that she write a "historical romance" in the manner of Walter Scott, she replied: "I could no more write a romance than an epic poem. I could not sit seriously down to write a serious romance under any other motive than to save my life; and if it were indispensible for me to keep it up and never relax into laughing at myself or other people, I am sure I should be hung before I had finished the first chapter. No, I must keep to my own style and go on in my own way; and though I may never succeed again in that, I am convinced that I should totally fail in any other." Not that Jane Austen was incapable of taking anything seriously; she could not take herself or her art seriously unless she was allowed to laugh or smile. Her novels are comedies not only because they are comic in spirit but because her temperament and dialectics were fundamentally ironical. They are comedies even in their structure and technique.

Her basic plots follow the time-tested technique of comedy—the obstacles and misunderstandings that must be overcome by lovers before they end by marrying each other. (It is a dramatic convention to call this a happy ending.) In her characterizations she relies to an unusually large extent on dialogue. She never, or hardly ever, describes her characters, preferring to let them talk as much as they like and thus unconsciously give themselves away (the illusion of their reality is created not by analysis or description but by their subtle interaction on one another, a secret she mastered more thoroughly than many a dramatist), and she observes the spirit of the classical rules of unity of time, place, and action—taking advantage of the latitude allowed to comedy. As in even the best of theatrical comedies, her denouements are the weakest part of her novels: to bring about a happy ending some *deus ex machina* is invariably required, whereas catastrophes come about quite naturally. Despite all this, her novels *are* novels, not plays in novel form. There have been dramatic adaptations of *Pride and Prejudice,* yet whatever their merits, they cannot do justice to the original. The reason is chiefly that, unlike works written for the stage, hers can gain nothing and indeed are likely to lose something by being represented physically. Her art consists in letting her characters come to life so completely, through the use of dramatic techniques, that the reader can realize them in his mind more vividly than any group of actors can impersonate them.

It is one thing to analyze the subtlety of Jane Austen's art or to explore some of the surprises that await him who probes her work beneath the surface; it is another thing to make anyone like her work if he is temperamentally uncongenial to it. Some may feel that an unconscionable amount of genius and ingenuity has been wasted for the sake of rather minuscule results, and one might say of Jane Austen what Voltaire said of Marivaux—that he laid insects' eggs in spider webs. True, the universe may be revealed in microcosms, but there are times when one does not feel in the mood for microcosms and prefers blatant crudity to concealed subtlety. Jane Austen herself once defined her work as a "little bit (two inches wide) of ivory on which I work with so fine a brush as produces little effect after much labor." Though exaggeratedly modest in most respects (and usually quoted to the

wrong purpose), her definition is true in a certain sense. And yet, few artists in any field who have restricted themselves to so limited an area as hers have approximated the universality and lastingness of her appeal. Many of her readers simply delight and rejoice in her style—which, incidentally, despite its elegance and limpidity, is by no means flawless: her novels abound in stilted sentences and very odd syntactical constructions (she is particularly addicted to unattached or ill-attached participles). An even larger segment of the reading public simply continues to be superlatively entertained by her and by the world she created, in spite of the fact that it is a completely vanished world. We still recognize ourselves and others in her characters, for the human comedy changes only in its settings and not in its cast of actors.

It was Mark Twain who defined a good library as one from which the works of Jane Austen were totally absent. Assuredly he did not mean to be taken literally or even quite seriously, but at any rate he made his feelings admirably clear and, by singling her out, paid her a handsome compliment. One can see how the utterly unsentimental and down-to-earth Miss Austen may have antagonized the author of *Personal Recollections of Joan of Arc.*

At the other extreme, Jane Austen has been praised somewhat extravagantly. A sense of proportion seems to be one of Miss Elizabeth Jenkins's outstanding qualities; yet she appears to have lost it when (in her otherwise admirable biography of Jane) she expresses quite unsmilingly her surprise that *Persuasion,* which would seem to "require a novel on the scale of *War and Peace*" to build up the fullness of its reality, is only "little longer than a long short story." Among short stories, *Persuasion* would seem an elephant if not a mammoth. It is true, however, that if Tolstoy in writing *War and Peace* had soberly decided to cut out all considerations philosophical and historical, skipped Austerlitz and Borodino, omitted all mention of Napoleon except for the effect his defeat and abdication produced on the real-estate market, and called it *Natasha* instead of *War and Peace,* he might have produced a book not too dissimilar to Jane Austen's novels. This statement is not meant altogether facetiously: in their simplicity, subtlety, tact, and economy, Tolstoy and Jane Austen had a great deal in common, and assuredly both were born writers. As artists they are probably equals, but their aims differed. Tolstoy would not have resented the comparison, but Miss Austen's modesty would have been as shocked as her sense of humor would have been tickled—and this is one of the many reasons why we love her.

J. Christopher Herold, a regular contributor to HORIZON, *wrote* The HORIZON Book of The Age of Napoleon, *published last fall.*

Evening the Score

DRAWINGS BY PAUL HORGAN

Paul Horgan, best known for his books on the Southwest and especially for his Pulitzer-prize-winning *Great River: The Rio Grande in North American History,* now reveals, for the first time in print, a thoroughly engaging talent for satirical drawing. "All my life," he says, "I have delighted in drawing and have met various occasions of ceremony, jubilee, or perhaps convalescence by drawing populations of creatures in series to amuse my friends." Here, and on the following two pages, we bring you his wicked population from the world of music, drawn as a Christmas present for an old friend, Rouben Mamoulian. During the twenties, when Mamoulian was a director at the Eastman Theatre in Rochester, New York, Horgan worked under him as an actor, singer, set designer, and writer. Perhaps Horgan's personal experience on the musical stage helped to provide the special, wry truth of these drawings.

Marguerite

German lieder: *der Umlaut*

Rhadames

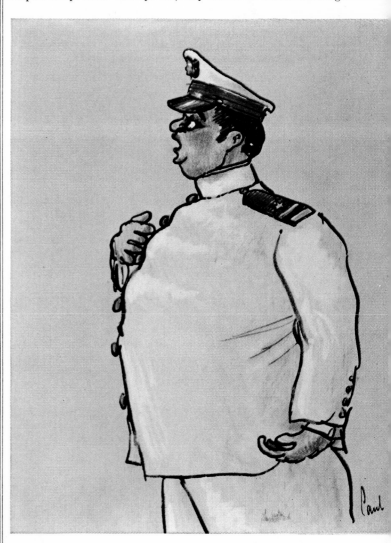

Lieutenant Pinkerton: *"O quanti occhi fissi . . ."*

Musicology at Harvard

The Convent Orchestra: *tempo di marcia*

ppp . . .

Italian opera: chorus master

Voice teacher:
the full round tone

Voice teacher: decrescendo

Prima donna assoluta

The Irish lyric tenor

Wunderkind

Concert entrance

The accompanist

51

After the war, Europe's damaged cities had to decide how to rebuild. Today the heart of Rotterdam is totally new and totally modern. In London, St. Paul's is now surrounded by a mixture of old and new. Only Warsaw has faithfully reproduced its old central quarter exactly as it was before the war.

Rotterdam

THE PHOENIX

A lesson in how to preserve and cherish the past comes, strangely enough, from behind the Iron Curtain

The end of World War II confronted many devastated cities in Europe and Asia with a problem: what to do about the relics of their past in rebuilding for the future. The experience of these cities—London, Coventry, and Rotterdam; Warsaw, Leningrad, and Hiroshima—is not without lessons for us who live elsewhere. For the uncontrolled erosion of peacetime construction threatens to wreak as much damage on the cities of the world as did the mindless violence of war. To the citizens of these phoenix cities, the war made diamond clear one fact which is often befogged in peace—namely, that the past is, in many real ways, the only material out of which we can build the future. The protection of historic districts, buildings, and works of art is thus not merely the task of museologists and antiquarians: it is the responsibility of every citizen who draws his sustenance, spiritual as well as economic, from the city.

With each city, of course, the problem varied. The old center of Rotterdam, completely leveled by high explosives, has been completely rebuilt along modern lines. London, heavily but spottily damaged by fire and blast, has tended to erect new buildings among the old within an essentially undisturbed street pattern. Coventry has entirely replaced her fire-swept business district with a remarkable new traffic-free commercial center. And instead of rebuilding her gutted Cathedral, she has made the empty shell into a walled garden and built a splendid modern church along the axis of the transepts. Leningrad has restored the rococo palaces along the Neva to their nineteenth-century splendor. Of prewar Hiroshima nothing remains but a twisted steel skeleton at "point zero" of the world's first atomic attack.

By JAMES MARSTON FITCH

London

FOX PHOTOS—PICTORIAL PARADE

Warsaw

EASTFOTO

CITIES OF POLAND

The special character of Poland's program for the reconstruction of her artistic and historic monuments derives from the special circumstances of her history, particularly the period of the Nazi occupation from 1939 to 1945. Many of her greatest cities, including Warsaw and Gdańsk (Danzig), and many of her villages were all but destroyed, their art looted and their historic buildings burned. Of course, other countries in Europe, including Germany herself, also endured great destruction. But no European city saw such coldly calculated demolition as Warsaw. She was the subject of four overwhelming attacks: first, in September, 1939; then, in the Battle of the Ghetto in 1943; again, in the Warsaw Uprising in 1944; and finally, in the Battle of Liberation of 1945. The naval and aerial bombardments of Gdańsk destroyed some 75 per cent of the medieval center of that great Hanseatic seaport, and laid waste one of the largest concentrations of late Gothic buildings in existence. Hence, the postwar problem in Poland has more often been reconstruction than mere preservation or restoration.

The question of how these cities were to be rebuilt was the subject of long and intensive discussion among Polish architects and town planners. Warsaw presented an especially complicated problem, psychologically as well as physically. As the historic capital of Poland and the center of Polish resistance, Hitler had ordered (in a famous telegram which now hangs in the Historical Museum) that it be leveled to the ground like Carthage and replaced by a small garrison town (the plan of which also hangs in the museum). The Poles felt that this barbarous act left them no possible choice but to reconstruct at least the *Stare Miasto,* the medieval walled center of the city, as it had been before the war. One cannot help feeling that they acted correctly: certainly, today, even members of the Polish architectural avant-garde who opposed the reconstruction at the time are agreed that the decision was correct.

The reconstruction of these historic areas is substantially complete. Elsewhere, in towns and villages which escaped destruction, the conservation of isolated buildings and complexes goes on apace. Here the problem is the more conventional one of preservation or restoration. The ancient city of Cracow, for example, escaped with little damage heavier than rifle fire. (The Nazis had systematically mined and wired it for demolition, but a lightning encirclement by Russian troops foiled this act of vandalism.) As a result, an artistic and historic treasure-trove remains intact. Like many provincial centers in the old Austro-Hungarian empire, Cracow saw little development during the eighteenth and nineteenth centuries. There were few of the urbanistic improvements that marked Vienna: long stretches of Cracow's medieval fortifications, for example, still encircle the city. As a result, there are whole areas of the old center that offer a comparatively undisturbed chronology of styles, from Romanesque to late-eighteenth-century rococo.

The care of all artistic and historic monuments in Poland is entrusted to the Ministry of Culture and Art. In this ministry there is a department which has jurisdiction over all museums and monuments. National programs and criteria for preservation work have been established by this central body, which has also drawn up an inventory of all such monuments and a sched-

Restoration of the older parts of Warsaw was aided by the meticulously painted streetscapes of an eighteenth-century itinerant from Italy, Bernardo Bellotto. Compare his painting of the Church of the Sisters of the Holy Sacrament at right with the various stages of its restoration below: as it was after the war, during reconstruction, and as it looks today. This church, like many others in Poland, was restored at government expense.

ule for undertaking rebuilding or repair. But the actual work is handled by regional offices.

Once a building has been declared a national monument, it cannot be altered by the owners without the permission of the national office. This, of course, is standard procedure in most countries where such agencies exist, as in France and Italy. But a peculiarity of Polish preservation work is that a building cannot be restored or reconstructed until a "client" is found to use it. Such a client may be a municipal agency, a school or museum, a national corporation, or a housing co-operative. An empty building in urgent need of physical repairs will be made weatherproof without having a client, but the interior will not be rebuilt or remodeled without one. However, national monuments in private ownership that are in urgent need of attention may be restored with government funds if the owners cannot afford to do it themselves. Many churches have been restored in this fashion.

Actually, no habitable building goes long untenanted. It is difficult for a Westerner to visualize how precious enclosed space is in a country like Poland. On the one hand, she lost millions of square feet of buildings in the course of six years of occupation and war. On the other, housing needs have increased enormously as has the need for factory and office space. Because of such absolute scarcity, the restoration and reconstruction of old buildings becomes much more feasible, economically, than it otherwise might be.

This policy leads to a certain amount of adaptation and alteration of historic buildings, which might disturb the purist

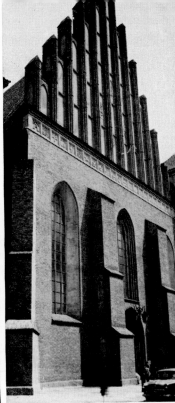

*Before bombing, Warsaw's
Cathedral of St. John wore a
flamboyant late-Gothic face
(left); in rebuilding it, an
earlier and severer style
of façade was restored (right).*

from the West. For example, the interiors of buildings which are located in old districts but which have, themselves, no prime importance either artistically or historically, are rebuilt along modern lines. The Poles point out that they would not want a landscape full of museums (like so many of the National Trust houses in England) even if they could afford them. Their policy, they claim, has the virtue of introducing life and movement into districts which might otherwise be dead. One has only to visit the Independence Hall district of Philadelphia, or the Mall in Washington, after dark to see the validity of their thesis.

In Polish architectural circles one hears many complaints about the low level of craftsmanship in the building industry. And it is very obvious, even to the visitor, that the workmanship in *new* construction leaves much to be desired. Modern Polish architects, like their colleagues in the West, aspire to a kind of formal perfectionism that is difficult to achieve even with the advanced technologies of the United States. (As a matter of fact, it has not proved particularly viable even here. Our identical use of the glass wall from Duluth to Miami, for example, is a grotesque abuse of function. And much of this slick, bright work, which depends for its aesthetic impact upon immaculate maintenance, ages much less gracefully than older, less "advanced" materials.) Be that as it may, there is little evidence of poor workmanship in Polish *preservation* work. Here the quality ranges from good to superlative. This may be partly due to the fact that, in nationally significant edifices like St. John's Cathedral or the Wilanów Palace the government was willing to concentrate funds and men on the project. This was

clearly the case in the newly opened National Opera House in Warsaw. An enormous enlargement of an old neoclassic building of the early nineteenth century, it will be not only the most complete opera plant in the world, but also one of the best built.

But another reason for the generally high level of preservation work is the fact that it involves many old-time luxury crafts which are no longer in demand in modern architecture—workers in marble, iron, and ornamental plaster; craftsmen in stained glass, and in wood and stone carving; gilders and painters. Since these skilled craftsmen are usually older men, few of them have been absorbed into the new industries. As in other Communist countries, such men have been sought out, organized into co-operative ateliers, and given jobs that derive from the preservation program.

Whatever the explanation, the restoration of such buildings as the Lazienki and Wilanów palaces in Warsaw is technically immaculate and visually dazzling. In them, the Polish experts faced a characteristic spectrum of problems. The Lazienki, small and all-of-a-piece, was gutted by Nazi demolition squads. Built by King Stanislas II Augustus in the last quarter of the eighteenth century, this elegant little rococo building stood in a downtown park and had long been open to the public. Hence it was possible and proper to restore it to its original state. That state was scintillating. Although designed by an Italian, Merlini, in the French manner, it bears the unmistakable *brio* and elegance of Polish taste. The architecture itself is fairly sober, but in the decoration—in the chocolate *rocaille* bathroom, the blue

55

and white delft tile boudoir, the pink and green marbelized rotunda, and the grotesque sculptures of the ballroom—one sees the wit and exuberance that marks the Pole.

The Wilanów Palace is a great château begun in 1677 and continuously lived in, altered, and redecorated until World War II. Deterioration of the physical fabric was due more to poor construction and simple neglect than to wartime damage. Since Wilanów had been designated as a museum of interior design and the decorative arts, the decision was very wisely made to restore different rooms or suites of rooms to different styles or periods. This has not always been easy, for it offers an embarrassment of riches: even minor rooms turn out to have several layers of frescoes, each of which is interesting historically if not artistically. The experts' problem is to decide at which layer to halt.

And, like many seventeenth- and eighteenth-century palaces, including Versailles itself, Wilanów turns out to have been very shoddily built. The restorers found startling structural weaknesses from foundations to attics; the whole fabric has had to be reinforced with new members in steel, concrete, or wood as circumstances required.

About half the palace has been restored and opened to the public; the rest is in process. When it is completed, the museum will offer a fascinating picture of almost three centuries of the domestic life of the Polish aristocracy. It is surprising, in this connection, to find the Communist countries lavishing so much attention—and all of it sympathetic—upon the re-creation of the homes of the old aristocracy. The results are misleadingly amiable. For to display these old palaces without all the squalid dependencies upon which they rested is to present as incomplete a picture of serfdom as do our bowdlerized restorations at Mt. Vernon and Monticello, where the odious facts of slavery have been virtually expunged from the picture. (When I asked why the peasant huts at Wilanów could not also be reconstructed, I was told it was too late: a model collective farm now occupies the site.) However, to give a more balanced picture of peasant life in the old days, several outdoor museums of the "Skansen type" (derived, that is, from the famous one in Stockholm) are under construction. The traditional houses, mills, barns, and chapels of the region will be assembled in a park, to give a picture of the life of the common people. There are also in preparation several so-called "museums of work" where various industries such as the ancient salt mines of Silesia will be re-created. (In addition, it should be pointed out that a vast program for the protection of the traditional arts and crafts of the common people is under way. One of the world's greatest libraries of folk music has been created in Warsaw, a network of regional ethnographic museums has been established to display all the folk arts of each region, and a broad program for the regeneration of the crafts and the integration of the craftsman into modern life is being carried out.)

Most Polish conservators follow the accepted international practice of insisting that a clear and visible distinction must always be maintained between original and new tissue in the fabric of a restored building. One outstanding exception is the

Some palaces and châteaux of the old aristocracy, like the Lazienki Palace (left), have been made into museums. This rococo palazzina in a Warsaw park was partially destroyed by the Nazis. The ruined boudoir (opposite) has been immaculately restored to its original state of Delft-tiled splendor.

fourteenth-century Collegium Maius in Cracow, which now houses a new university museum. Although the restorer, Dr. Karol Estreicher, insists that he disapproves of Viollet-le-Duc, a detached observer can scarcely fail to see certain resemblances between the work of the two men. (Viollet-le-Duc was a nineteenth-century French architect-cum-archaeologist who restored Notre-Dame and Sainte-Chapelle in Paris and the walled city of Carcassonne in southern France to the state in which we see them today. His policy of deciding, on the basis of personal taste alone, which period to re-create is in disrepute today.)

Dr. Estreicher thinks that distinctions between old and new tissue are of interest only to experts, and that such information is much better preserved in the archives than in the building itself; he believes that the restorer should use all his talent to create a convincing picture of the selected period. It must be admitted that the half-finished restoration of Collegium Maius offers persuasive support for his argument. The completed galleries afford an ingratiating background for the university collection of paintings, *objets d'art,* and furniture. Since the Collegium had been gutted by fire during World War II, he had nothing but an empty, roofless shell to work with. And since the building was to be rebuilt as a museum (it had previously been used for classes), certain liberties had to be taken. The restorer's approach in this case may be defensible, but as a general policy for conservation it is clearly hazardous—one that is certain to cause trouble for future conservators and curators.

But the aspect of Polish conservation work which is at once the most impressive and the most controversial is the *recon-struction* of vanished buildings. In Warsaw the whole of the medieval center has been rebuilt in facsimile, as well as the mile-long stretch of Krakowskie Przedmiescie and Nowy Swiat that runs along the bluffs above the Vistula River. In Gdańsk one of the three medieval enclaves has been reproduced in this way, including many of the old port buildings, the City Hall, the Cathedral of Saint Mary, and numerous Gothic monuments which lie outside this area. These reconstructions have been the subject of many polemics, abroad as well as inside Poland. Generally speaking, the younger architects, artists, and intelligentsia have been opposed. Even the architect who was in charge of the Stare Miasto reconstruction confesses that he had private reservations about it at the time.

Events have fully confirmed the validity of the policy. The reasons for its success, however, are not primarily aesthetic: they are political, patriotic, emotional. Observers from the West must see the documentary evidence—photographs and movies, many of them prepared by the Germans themselves—to have any comprehension of conditions in Warsaw immediately before and after liberation. The city had been reduced to a lunar wasteland. The destruction involved not only buildings, streets, and utilities but all cultural artifacts: even monuments of national heroes like Copernicus, Chopin, the nineteenth-century poet Mickiewicz, and Poniatowski, Napoleon's general, had been destroyed. In a very real sense such political destruction left only one political response: complete restoration. Above and beyond that, in the first years after the war, living under con-

Cracow suffered only minor damage in the war; all its old buildings, in many architectural styles, came through unscathed. The fifteenth-century barbican tower (background) and the earlier St. Florian's Gate (foreground) are parts of the medieval fortifications which even today surround most of the inner town of this former Polish capital.

ditions of incredible hardship, the people of Warsaw needed psychological security as much as physical shelter. The restoration of familiar streetscapes and beloved landmarks was thus a matter of fundamental importance to the restoration of the life of the city.

Even today, with the city largely rebuilt and tens of thousands of new apartments in new neighborhoods on both banks of the Vistula, the Stare Miasto is a favorite neighborhood for artists and professional people. It has the most active night life in the capital. Aside from historic associations, the narrow picturesque old streets and cosy little squares of the quarter apparently afford a more hospitable setting for street life than the spacious avenues and extensive parks of the new city.

In Gdańsk the reasons for restoring the old quarters were perhaps more archaeological than emotional. The city never had a significance in Polish history comparable to Warsaw's, and its destruction was almost incidental to military logistics: as an important seaport it was a target for air attack, and much of the destruction came from allied bombs. On the other hand, the great churches, burghers' houses, guild halls and warehouses, done in the fantastic brick Gothic idiom of the Hanseatic League, were perhaps more significant architecturally than anything in Warsaw. So here again the decision was made to reconstruct at least part of it in facsimile. In both cities these facsimile reconstructions are largely exterior. The main intent is to restore the streetscape. Except for monumental public buildings, the interiors have been replanned and rebuilt along quite modern lines, with all modern amenities including district heat-

ing. (Both of these cities have giant thermoelectric plants that furnish heat, light, and power to the entire town. An admirable system which all but eliminates the heavy coal smoke that is the curse of northern Europe, it will ultimately be used in all Polish towns.)

Of course, the greater part of both cities has been rebuilt along contemporary town-planning principles, with wide streets, lavish park and green spaces, modern boulevard and highway systems, zoned land use, and so on. But in such brand-new cityscapes, handsome as they often are, isolated old buildings of no special artistic merit achieve great visual and emotional significance. Such landmarks help the visitor in orienting himself; to the natives they are cherished mementos. In Warsaw, for example, a lightly damaged (and mediocre) rococo church was bodily moved some fifty yards to make way for the widening of a street. And a battle-scarred fragment of the Unknown Soldier's Tomb, of no intrinsic merit in itself, has been carefully worked into a landscaped park.

In the restoration or reconstruction of historic buildings the Polish conservationists—like such experts everywhere—often face the necessity of deciding to what stage of its history a given structure should be "returned." In the case of Warsaw's eighteenth-century Church of the Sisters of the Holy Sacrament, which had been built as a unit and never subsequently altered, reconstruction posed no problems. But sometimes, in old and complex structures, the decisions are surprising. For example, in Warsaw's St. John's Cathedral, the flamboyant Gothic façade

Gdansk (left), on the Baltic, one of the late-Gothic cities of the Hanseatic League, was repeatedly bombed. Its gutted Town Hall and burghers' mansions have been restored to mint condition. The Cathedral of St. Mary (below) now looks down on rows of storybook town houses. Behind the restored façades are modern flats with municipal steam heat and all conveniences.

(late but wonderfully picturesque) was not reconstructed: instead, a much earlier and more severe stepped gable was recreated (see page 55). When it comes to making such decisions, the Poles seem always to have extensive documentation at hand. And this is all the more remarkable in view of the ravaged museums, libraries, and archives of World War II. In Warsaw proper, architectural students at the Polytechnic had for years been required to make measured drawings of old buildings in the Stare Miasto; these largely survived. This type of work was carried on, all during the Nazi occupation, by the Underground University, which also laid the basic outlines of the new plan of Warsaw. Among the most useful documents in the reconstruction of Warsaw (as also in Dresden) were the paintings of Bernardo Bellotto, who worked in Warsaw in the 1760's–70's. His views of various sites have proved so accurate that they are used by the conservationists as guides to vanished monuments.

The work of restoring Poland's historic monuments is today, eighteen years after the war, possibly 80 per cent complete. And the visitor from the West can only marvel at the scope of this work and praise it for its uniformly high quality. A past so cherished will offer valuable guide lines to future action not only in Poland but elsewhere in the world.

James Marston Fitch, professor of architecture at Columbia University, is the author of Architecture and the Esthetics of Plenty. *He has recently been studying the preservation of historic buildings in Europe, the Middle East, and Africa.*

A
BANNER
YEAR
FOR BANNERS

A number of late-Victorian social critics spent the better part of their idealistic lives calling for a return to the principles of the Middle Ages. Then, as legend has it—or as they thought—artist and craftsman worked together in mutual respect, the horrors of mass production were undreamed of, and life was colored by the kind of pageantry represented by the resplendent herald above. Of course it wasn't like that at all, but those who wish it were can take some comfort in the news that a group of New York avant-garde painters and a retinue of Seventh Avenue seamstresses have joined talents to revive a tradition that dates back to the thirteenth century. Together, they are producing the most rousing set of banners seen anywhere since the Battle of Agincourt.

This intersection of art circles and sewing circles began during the 1963 newspaper strike; the Graham Gallery, at a loss to publicize an exhibition of abstractionist Alfred Jensen's work, had the artist paint a huge flag to fly outside the building. The banner was

Alfred Jens

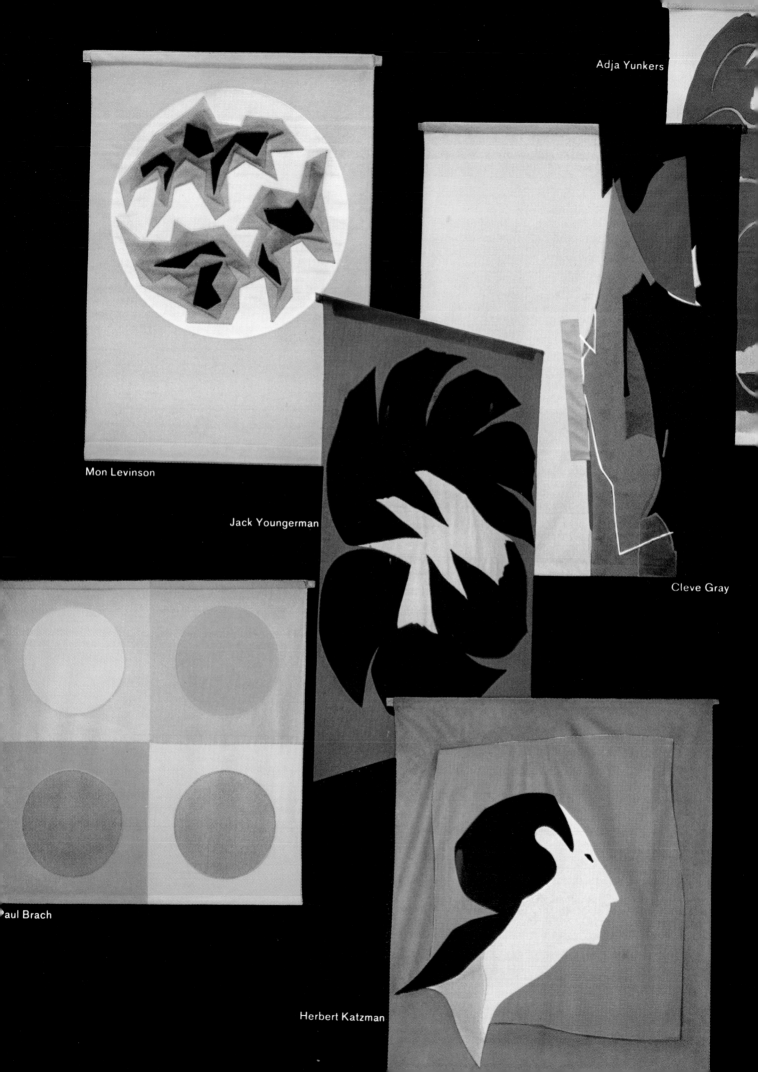

Mon Levinson

Jack Youngerman

Adja Yunkers

Cleve Gray

Paul Brach

Herbert Katzman

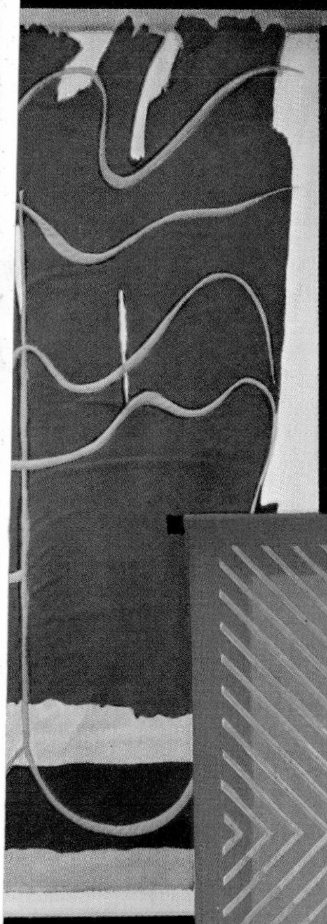

Richard Anuszkiewicz

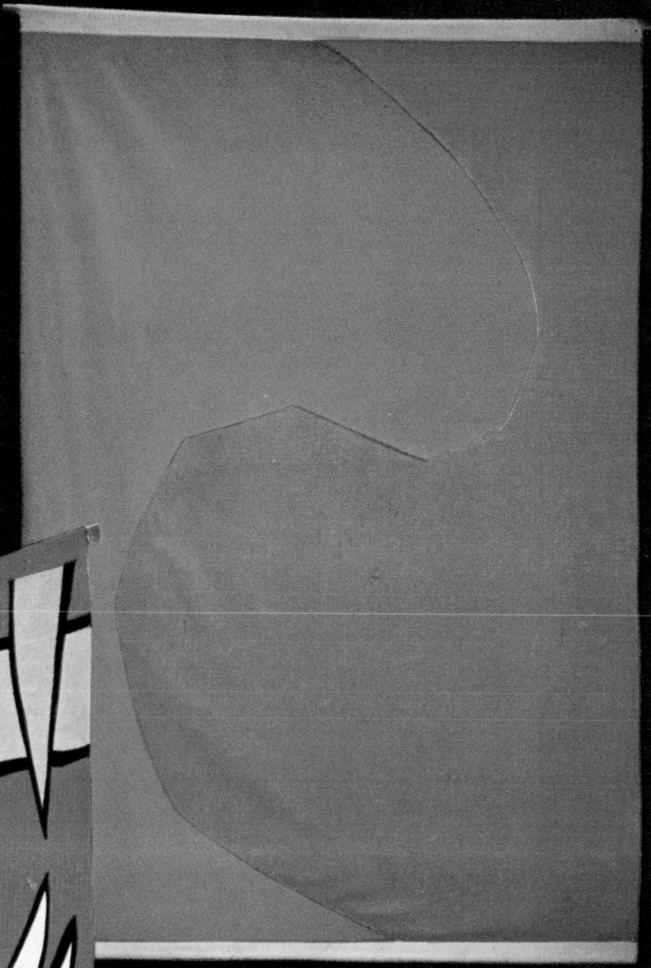

Leon Polk Smith

Nicholas Krushenick

George Ortman

T

By PETER FRYER

IN
B—D
WITH
MRS.
GRUNDY

It is often said that Mrs. Grundy is today far less of a busybody, and in any case far less influential, than she used to be; and certainly young people are willing to put up with much less from her than their predecessors seem to have done, so that to most of them her name now means little.* Nevertheless she remains (though going on 170) a pretty energetic and persistent old person, who very much wants to regain her influence over people's lives. Nor is there any guarantee that she will not succeed.

Of her activities today there is plenty of evidence. There was the case of the young woman undergraduate who was expelled from her university after being found in bed with a man; it is a characteristic stroke of Grundyism that the man was able to purge *his* offense with merely a two-week suspension. There was the London bookseller who refused to display copies of a book whose jacket bore a drawing of a naked young man by William Blake. There was the London composer who sought to prosecute the B.B.C. for broadcasting—for the seventh time since 1954—the "obscene" sixteenth-

* Mrs. Grundy is a fictional character of rare persistence. She originated in a play by Thomas Morton called *Speed the Plough,* which was first produced in 1798. Two of the characters in the play are farmers' wives, Mrs. Ashfield and Mrs. Grundy. Although the latter never shows her face on stage, she is seldom far from Mrs. Ashfield's thoughts—for that worthy lady is constantly wringing her hands and crying "What will Mrs. Grundy say?" From this invisible beginning, Mrs. Grundy has grown to represent—always in a disapproving sense, of course—Anglo-Saxon propriety and morality.

century play *Gammer Gurton's Needle.* In Lebanon, one of the lands where belly dancers have for decades been observed with interest by tourists and other students of folk culture, the authorities decreed the prohibition of a new American dance, the twist. Before long the London Dance Institute followed suit, on the ground that the dance was "far too uninhibited, abandoned, and frankly sexy to be performed in Britain." Meanwhile in Saigon a kinswoman of Mrs. Grundy was inspiring an austerity law prohibiting private or commercial dancing, cabarets, and beauty contests; while in Los Angeles her American cousin was prompting members of a local school board to consider banning all Tarzan books from

young people's libraries, because of a complaint that Tarzan and his mate Jane were apparently living in their jungle tree-house without benefit of clergy. At a hospital in Chesterfield, England, nurses were ordered to lengthen the skirts of their uniforms so as not to show their knees; if their skirts were any higher, said the matron, "patients would see the girls' stocking tops when they bent down to tuck in the sheets." Precisely how this would impair the patients' recovery she did not reveal.

Prudery is fear and hatred of pleasure, primarily of sexual pleasure; and Mrs. Grundy is a prude who carries this fear and hatred to the stage of more or less organized interference with other people's pleasures. The private prude and the prude-at-large are both obsessed by an awareness of the vast amount of unregulated pleasure that is being enjoyed in the world; this they call sin. When they inveigh or organize against sin they are consciously or unconsciously buttressing their own inner barriers against the pleasure they long for but fear to obtain. Sometimes their extreme shockability and militancy are pharisaical; but it is only a minority of prudes who are hypocrites. The majority are unaware of their real motives. To a healthy person the sexual behavior of others may be of interest, but it is not an obsession; he can contemplate without distress forms of pleasure and fulfillment that do not correspond to his own habits and tastes, provided those forms do not infringe upon the freedom of choice of mature persons or the inviolability of the immature. To the prude and to Mrs. Grundy, however, the sexual activity of others is simultaneously inflammatory and disgusting, and of such obsessive interest that it is rarely far from their thoughts. It stimulates their imaginations and inventive powers. "The dreaded subject," says one of the most sensible writers on prudery, "is detected in a thousand innuendoes, in inanimate as well as animate forms." It is a constant and fascinating reminder of their own frustration and unhappiness; it perpetually awakens feelings whose existence they spend their lives denying and trying to suppress; it impels them to punish both their tormentors and themselves.

The prude-in-authority becomes a censor, whose function is to protect his fellow men against images which he considers indecent and immoral, depraving and corrupting—especially against descriptions of sexual activity which present it as something pleasurable. Those the censor protects are put in the position of children being guarded from harm. They may not read books that someone else considers unsuitable; nor see plays or motion pictures before someone else has seen them and dictated whatever cuts he deems necessary; nor (at times) see certain paintings or pieces of sculpture that might, in the opinion of someone else, arouse sexual desire. The prude-in-office himself is supposed to be impervious to the harmful influence of the mass of erotic material it is his distasteful duty to examine. Moreover the existence of even the most stringent censorship has never prevented the publication and distribution of large numbers of erotic books and pictures. Eroticism in art and literature is as old as art and literature themselves; which seems to show that prudes, with or without law-enforcement officers to help them, have little chance of ever making sex uninteresting.

Prudery's first line of defense is the regulation of speech. Feelings of shame and guilt about the organs of sexual activity, and other bodily functions, tend to become closely associated with the words that are used for them. Then these words become taboo, and other words come into use, free from the emotions that now suffuse the original terms. As often as not, the new words themselves are felt sooner or later to have become tainted and to need replacement. By its very nature, euphemism tends to lose its protective magic at a fairly rapid rate.

The high point in the use of euphemism was reached in 1833 when Noah Webster, the famous lexicographer, got down to the task of bowdlerizing the Bible (even cutting out whole verses "as beyond the reach of effective bowdlerization"). Although the First World War brought about a partial return to plain speaking, prudish modes of speech clung on tenaciously among some groups. For instance, in the thirties the Hollywood list of banned words, which might never be spoken in any motion picture, included "cocotte," "courtesan," "eunuch," "harlot," "madam" (for brothel-keeper), "slut," "tart," "trollop," "wench," "whore," "son-of-a-bitch," "sex," and "sexual." The words "virtuous" and "bum" were to be avoided, and the expression "traveling salesman" might not be used "where reference is made to a farmer's daughter."

Of the making of euphemisms there is indeed—alas for the delicately minded who need them—no end. Once a euphemism becomes accepted and its primary meaning changes to the shameful thing for which it has come to stand, the taboo, if it be strong enough, tends to be transferred. The goose flesh reappears. And some fresh, innocent victim-word has to be sacrificed on the altar of propriety. The results are often laughable. Or rather, the euphemisms of past generations strike us as comical; our own simply show how polite we are, and how considerate of other people's feelings.

The words that designate the parts of the body or those that describe nakedness have always alarmed Mrs. Grundy. Nearly half a century ago H. L. Mencken hit on the ingenious idea of arranging the parts of the body in an "inte-rior hierarchy" of eight classes, beginning with the highly respectable ones and ending with what in 1915 were regarded as unmentionable. Class I consisted of the heart, brain, hair, eyes, and vermiform appendix, "five aristocrats, of dignity even in their diseases." Class II included the collarbone, the stomach (in America) and liver (in England), the bronchial tubes, arms (excluding elbows), tonsils, ears, cheeks, and chin. Descending to Class III, one had the elbows, ankles, teeth (if natural), shoulders, lungs, neck, etc. In Class IV came the stomach (in England) and liver (in America), hips, calves, nose, feet (bare), etc. Teeth (if false), heels, toes, knees, legs (female), and scalp were grouped in Class V; thighs, paunch, esophagus, spleen, pancreas, gall bladder, and caecum in Class VI. Mencken omitted to name the constituents of his two other classes, VII and VIII, because these "entered into anatomical details impossible of discussion in a book designed to be read aloud at the domestic hearth."

In 1936 a woman lunatic took off her clothes in St. Paul's Cathedral. The *Daily Express, Daily Mail,* and *Daily Telegraph,* in their reports of the incident, described her as "unclothed." The *Daily Herald* called her "nude" in a headline, but elsewhere used "unclothed." The *News Chronicle* had "unclothed" and "unclad." Not one single daily newspaper was able to face the horror of the decent old English word "naked."

First recorded in the ninth century, this word, along with "bare" (before the year 1000), was almost ousted by "nude" (1873) in the nineteenth; though, strangely enough, the Latin word *nudus,* from which "nude" is directly derived, is a cousin-word of "naked." Yet "naked" was felt to be too stark long before the nineteenth century, it seems. For in Wycherley's *The Country Wife* (acted circa 1672), when Sir Jaspar Fidget says, "Faith to tell you the naked truth," his wife reproves him: "Fye, Sir *Jaspar,* do not use that word naked." Those who, like Lady Fidget, have found verbal nakedness an affront to their susceptibilities have had plenty of euphemisms at their disposal: "uncovered" (c. 1400), "unclad" (c. 1420), "unrigged" (late sixteenth century), "in buff" (seventeenth century) and "stripped to the buff" (nineteenth century), "in birthday gear" (1731) and "in birthday attire" (1860), "peeled" (1820), "in the altogether" (1894), "starkers" (c. 1910; Oxford University slang) and "starko" (c.1910), and "in a state of nature."

One of the earliest victims of verbal prudery was "belly" (1340), very gradually replaced by "stomach" (c. 1375). Respectable Englishwomen used to be shocked if a Continental physician asked them whether the pain they complained of was in the belly; one foreign physician practicing in Britain was told in 1900 that his blunt use of that "dreadful" word had affected a female patient most unpleasantly. "Belly-ache" (before 1552; standard English till c. 1800) became "stomach-ache" (1763) and even "gastrodynia" (1804) and "gastralgia" (1822) and, later, "a pain in one's pinny." No one seems to have thought of saying "stomach-laugh"; but *The Stomach Dance* is the title of an illustration by Aubrey Beardsley for the first English edition of Wilde's *Salome* (1894). Eventually the more modest speakers found even "stomach" too coarse for their stomachs—Anthony Trollope let his publisher change "fat stomach" to "deep chest" in *Barchester Towers* (1857)—and descended to "tum" and "tummy" (1868), "tum-tum" (before 1904), and *little Mary* (1903, from Barrie's play of that name).

The word "leg" seems to have engendered still more distress than "belly," especially in the United States, where even "feet" was banned at one time, and where, as is well known, the legs of pianofortes were solemnly dressed in frilly trousers to keep the very thought of legs out of people's minds.

There is a story about a young American woman, injured in an accident, who told the surgeon one of her limbs was broken. He asked her which limb it was. "I can't tell you, doctor," she replied, "but it's one of my limbs." "Which is it," the doctor demanded, "the limb you thread a needle with?" "No, sir," she answered with a sigh, "it's the limb I wear a garter on." And Longfellow, in *Kavanagh* (1849), quotes from the prospectus of a fashionable American boarding school: "Young ladies are not allowed to cross their 'benders' in school."

Women's "breasts" had always been known as their "bosoms"; the two words were both first recorded about the year 1000. But in the early part of the nineteenth century the first became indelicate, and in America even the breast of a turkey was referred to as its bosom, as Thomas Marryat notes in his novel *Peter Simple* (1834):

It was my fate to sit opposite to a fine turkey, and I asked my partner if I should have the pleasure of helping her to a piece of the breast. She looked at me very indignantly, and said, "Curse your impudence, sar, I wonder where you larn manners. Sar, I take a lilly turkey *bosom* if you please."

At the close of the eighteenth century the garments that lay next to legs, belly, buttocks, and breast began to share the taboo that was more and more coming to surround these parts of the body. For instance, the original terms for the garments covering the lower half of a man's body were "breeches" (before 1000) and "trousers" (1681). Eighteenth-century delicacy replaced these words with the euphemism "inexpressibles," closely followed by "indescribables" (1794), "unmentionables" (1836), "sit-down-upons" (1840), "indispensables" (1841), and "unhintables" (before 1904). Other words peculiar to America were "conveniences," "nether integuments," and "femoral habiliments."

Indispensable these garments undoubtedly were to the mid-nineteenth-century gentleman; but if we had only Mrs. Beeton as a guide to his dress, we should have to conclude that he did not wear them. For that famous authority on household management, describing in 1861 the duties of a good valet, tells how he presents the various articles of the toilet as they are wanted, and then "the body-linen, neck-tie . . . waistcoat, coat, and boots, in suitable order, and carefully brushed and polished.

Having thus seen his master dressed . . ." The trousers were literally unmentionable.

At times the very mention of "underclothing" has been taboo. In the 1860's the *Washington Union* dared not advertise shirts and men's drawers under any bolder heading than "Gentlemen's Belongings." In 1898 the *Ladies' Home Journal* announced that it would in future avoid all reference to women's underwear, since "the treatment of the subject in print calls for minutiae of detail which is extremely and pardonably offensive to refined and sensitive women."

The prude's attention is also easily engaged by outer clothing, especially the clothing of women. It is a commonplace that the changes in women's fashions are basically determined by the need to maintain men's sexual interest, and therefore to transfer the primary zone of erotic display once a given part of the body has been saturated with attractive power to the point of satiation. The prude finds each new, revealing fashion a profoundly shocking and disturbing experience. He cannot tear his eyes away from the ankles, or knees, or breasts, or backs, or buttocks, with which the world around him is suddenly filled. Others are pleased and amused for a time by the fresh evidence that women have both shapes and wiles; but the prude, fleeing from his own erethism, defends his peace of mind by attacking the new fashion as indecent and immoral.

There even came a time, in the nineteenth century, when Mrs. Grundy persuaded the designers of valentines to put Cupid in a skirt, caused women to bathe in garments that took fully twelve yards of material, and rendered one bride so appalled by the sight of her husband's legs when he wore his nightshirt that she spent her honeymoon "making him nice long nightgowns so that I shan't be able to see any of him."

Prudery about covering parts of the body, however, is seldom consistent. Under Queen Victoria, evening dress was the exception to the general rule that women's clothes must hide their figures.

In evening dress a woman might exploit the top half of her breasts. But always there was the ladylike assumption that any results therefrom were unsought for and were ordained by a Higher Hand. The condemnatory words "bold," "fast," and "immodest" signified that the offender had used her gifts designedly. Thus when a famous Paris fashion house made an evening dress for one exceptionally proper young woman, she had her maid fill in the deep V with a modest fichu of lace and tulle and add short sleeves. "Nothing remains exposed," commented a wit, "save the fact that she is a virgin."

It is an easy step—by Grundyite logic —from disapproving of the revealing ball gown to disapproving of dancing itself. The prude finds the public embracing of men and women in the dance intolerably suggestive. The dance is in one sense a mimetic representation of copulation, and, as such, a form of courtship. It presents itself to the prude not as an innocent enjoyment but as a kind of licensed *frottage*. The horror expressed in England when the waltz was first introduced there is a good example.

The waltz came to England from Germany in 1812 and was immediately opposed as indecorous—largely because the dancers embraced as they danced. Mothers forbade their daughters to dance in this improper way; many people viewed the waltz as an attempt to shake the foundations of society; and there was talk of getting up a petition to Parliament for its prohibition as a national danger. Nevertheless the new dance, "an outright romp . . . as destitute of figure or variety as the motion of a horse in a mill," became a national craze. In the *Sporting Magazine* a correspondent signing himself "Hop" denounced this "will-corrupting dance" as a compound of immodest gesture and infectious poison, and recommended that the "disgusting interloper" be sent back to Germany.

One of the first anti-waltzing satires was written by Byron, though how far his tongue was in his cheeck may be judged from the pseudonym he adopted: Horace Hornem, Esq. The new dance,

he wrote, "wakes to wantonness the willing limbs." Not even Cleopatra had "displayed so much of *leg*, or more of *neck*," while

Round all the confines of the yielded waist,
The strangest hand may wander undisplaced.

The author of *The Ladies' Pocket-Book of Etiquette* (1840) devoted ten stern pages to "the pollution of the waltz," which she characterized as an anti-English dance, "the most degenerating . . . that the last or present century can see." "Ask the mother . . . can she consent to commit her daughter promiscuously to the arms of each waltzer? . . . Ask the lover . . . could he endure the sight of the adopted of his heart half-embraced and all but reclining in the arms of another? . . . Ask the husband . . . Will you suffer your wife to be half-embraced by every puppy who can turn on his heel or his toe?" Obviously, Mrs. Grundy found the waltz intolerable.

Nor has this tight-lipped lady always limited her censure to people's pleasures. She has also carried the body taboo into the field of medicine. For instance, the prude may not approve of his wife being examined by a male physician. He may even object to his baby being delivered by a male obstetrician. In fact, the lengths to which medical delicacy has been carried can seem quite extraordinary to a non-Grundyite.

A great lady of Middlesex lay in labor. The midwife thought it advisable to call in a physician; so Dr. Willughby of Derby was sent for. At the door of the lady's chamber he paused, crouched down—and crept into the room on hands and knees, so as to examine his patient unperceived. His examination over, he crept out again in the same way.

This happened in 1658. Not for another hundred years or more was it thought proper for male physicians to attend women in childbirth. Even when it did become the custom for qualified men to help bring children into the world, such men had to grope in the dark, underneath the bedclothes.

Delivering babies blindly in this way was a hazardous undertaking. Operating

under the bedclothes on one occasion, the great William Smellie, "the Master of British Midwifery," accidentally divided the umbilical cord in the wrong place, which resulted in a copious hemorrhage. With notable resource he seized and retied the cord, then won the admiration of the hitherto censorious midwife by telling her that was his way of preventing convulsions in the child. He said afterward that he had never been so frightened in his life.

Between prurient critics and prudish patients, the medical profession did not have too enviable a time of it. The lives of innumerable women were lost through what Havelock Ellis called fossilized modesty, "a kind of pseudo-modesty which, being a convention and not a natural feeling, is capable of unlimited extension." A coroner wrote in 1908 that he had known several cases of female deaths, reported as sudden and of cause unknown, when the medical man called in during the latter hours of life was quite unaware that his patient was dying of gangrene or of a strangulated femoral hernia. For women would sometimes hide their symptoms out of a bashfulness "so great and perverse as to be hardly credible."

Fortunately this particularly lethal form of prudishness has almost disappeared. And now—in 1964—we seem to ourselves to live in a period of relative enlightenment and tolerance. There is, however, no reason to assume that Mrs. Grundy is incapable of returning to a position of influence. Even today, it is as well not to be too boastful about our attitudes to other people's pleasures. It is easy to laugh at the prudery of former generations; it is far from easy to detect our own, which we are in the habit of calling good taste.

Peter Fryer, formerly an English newspaperman, has written books on Hungary and Portugal. This article, in slightly different form, will appear in Mrs. Grundy, *the first of two books the author has planned on English prudery. It will be published in America by London House and Maxwell later this month.*

Mantegna
of Mantua

The Gonzagas, as Mantegna portrayed them in the Camera degli Sposi at Mantua, so perfectly embody the dignity and reserve of their court painter's style that it is hard to tell how much is Gonzaga, how much Mantegna. He spent forty-eight years in their service,

His manner was prickly, his life was mundane

and methodical, his painting was poised and

static; why then should he have so much power

to move us? But that is the miracle of art

Mantegna: the first associations are hardness, intensity, brilliance. Already we have begun to describe a jewel— a ruby or an emerald—or a polished stone, perhaps agate. And Mantegna's art is as ornamental, as elegant, as these in spite of its fierceness. It is a monumentally static art—gigantic, yet with a jewel's exotic and irreducible character of something transformed from baser materials into a final rare and precious substance.

Andrea Mantegna was born in 1431 and died in 1506, which means that his life spanned seventy-five years of one of the most adventurous centuries in the history of art. As a child prodigy, he was exposed to the new thought of the early Renaissance in Italy and its expression in the new art. The physical world was being discovered with eager curiosity. Art responded with a realism that was based— technically—on the scientific investigation of anatomy and perspective. The classical past was also being rediscovered, and artists tried to emulate its sensuous idealism in forms derived from its broken sculpture and its ruined architecture. These were the elements of a revolutionary art—but at the same time, art continued its revelation of a Christian mystery that contradicts both the reality of the world around us and the pagan world of Greece and Rome.

In the fusion of these disparate elements no artist surpassed Mantegna in power and conviction, or in technical mastery. With his magnificent, hard-bitten style he is one of the greatest artists of a century that produced more great artists than any before or since.

Mantegna was born the son of a carpenter in Isola de Cartura, but as a small child he was adopted by a painter named Squarcione who had a workshop in Padua. Squarcione is no great figure as an artist nor, from what we can deduce, was he much of a person, and the adoption was not a matter of affection but a practical measure to bind an apprentice to a master. Adoptions of this sort were usual enough for artists or craftsmen who had no sons of their own to train, and Squarcione had several such apprentices, some of whom, including Mantegna, finally had to appeal to the law to sever a connection that was disproportionately profitable to their master.

By all accounts Mantegna became, in effect, the master teacher of Squarcione's workshop. But if he learned little from Squarcione directly, the workshop was a clearinghouse for new ideas brought to provincial Padua by painters and sculptors from Florence, already a Renaissance city. Although the University of Padua was still essentially medieval, its humanists, who apparently respected Squarcione as an antiquarian, were eager to absorb the new learning. The workshop was a meeting place where artists and scholars discussed classical fragments and classical literature with the intensity once reserved for holy relics and the Bible.

By the time he was eighteen Mantegna was receiving substantial commissions. At twenty-three he married Nicolosia, the daughter of Jacopo Bellini, the leading Venetian painter. At twenty-five, a highly paid artist of established reputation, he dissolved his contract with Squarcione. At this time he might have gone wherever he pleased, but two years later, in the crucial decision of his life, he entered the service of Lodovico Gonzaga of Mantua, and remained attached to the ducal court for the rest of his life—nearly half a century.

Although he could, and did, travel to the great centers when he wished, his attachment to a provincial court meant that he was more of a spectator than a participant in the movements that transformed art from then on. But it also meant that his own art developed with a consistency, a strength, and an individuality unmodified by the philosophical questioning that affected artists in Florence and Rome. Mantegna remained an artist of the early Renaissance in the fullest expression of its youthful vigor, but he brought to it the mature power of a lifework that advanced steadily and confidently in a single direction.

If the court of the Gonzagas in Mantua was provincial in

By JOHN CANADAY

comparison with the splendid and aggressive courts in Venice, Florence, and Rome, it was still the perfect court for Mantegna. The Gonzagas, of all possible patrons, seem to have shared most closely his own characteristics. Their tradition was stern, reserved. Yet as Renaissance humanists they were fascinated by a romantic vision of the classical past and were avid for learning, not as a path to social grace, but because they felt an identification between their own vigor and the vigor of an ancient Roman world that they envisioned in heroic terms, a military pageant at a celestial level. The Gonzagas had a fine sense of the theatrical on a grand scale, and so did Mantegna. Like Mantegna, they made up in masculine energy what they lacked in feminine sensitivity, in strength what they lacked in a taste for contemplation, in alertness what they lacked in subtlety.

If this identification of the Gonzagas' character with the style of Mantegna's painting seems too pat, the reason is that we can never visualize the family except as Mantegna showed them in their portraits, assembled along the walls of the Camera degli Sposi in the ducal castle. Any artist who is more than a hack paints something of himself into his portraits of no matter whom; he frequently tells you more about himself than about his sitters. But Mantegna's association with the Gonzagas was too long and its course, over-all, too harmonious to have been based on anything but a response between sympathetic natures. Hence if we have turned the Gonzagas into Mantegnas, surely any error is only one of degree.

Were there ever people more firm, more assured in their sense of power without arrogance, more calm in the face of inspection, more aware of the presence of the observer without admitting him to their confidence, than the Gonzagas as Mantegna shows them in the Camera degli Sposi? Each one of them is a monument to himself. Each exists with a decisiveness and an assurance that puts the word "dignity" beside the point. They are hard, strong, and vital—adjectives perfectly descriptive of Mantegna's art—and while they are united to one another in unquestioning conviction of the ends they share, each holds himself apart as a man responsible first to himself.

Mantegna, too, was an individualist—one of the great individualists in the history of art. We may trace his apparent debts to other artists and point out that his preoccupations with perspective, anatomy, and the classical past were common to all Italian artists of his century. But essentially he stands alone, individualistic in his use of these discoveries. He is so isolated that he is often misjudged, misinterpreted because he cannot be understood by the standards applicable to his contemporaries in other, more prolific schools of Renaissance art.

The most devoted lovers of Florentine art complain that as a stylist Mantegna lacks the breadth and freedom and, as an expressive artist, the human warmth that the Tuscans offer. They cannot see that Mantegna's rejection of move-

Part fortress and part residence, the Gonzagas' medieval castle (top) is more suggestive of the family's rise to power as local war lords than of the humanistic court sponsored by Lodovico Gonzaga and reflected by Mantegna in the frescoes of the so-called Camera degli Sposi (above). Probably a dining room, its walls present a family pageant in which courtiers, scholars, poets, and retainers all join to welcome home a son who has become a cardinal. The scene is rich, but more ceremonial than truly festive. The visit took place in 1472; Mantegna completed work on the frescoes two years later.

Not all of the participants shown on the walls of the Camera degli Sposi are identifiable with certainty today. The likelihood that Mantegna would have included his self-portrait as an important member of the Gonzagas' entourage, plus a strong resemblance to a bronze head known to be a portrait of Mantegna in old age, seems to justify identification of the central figure in the detail above as the artist. While the Gonzagas were congregated along the walls with their contemporary humanists, the classical past they worshiped was represented on the ceiling. Medallion portraits of Roman emperors, and spandrels telling stories from classical mythology, were incorporated in an illusionistic architectural scheme that made the ceiling—which is actually flat—seem to curve upward toward a central orifice opening on a painted sky.

In 1448, at the age of seventeen, Mantegna was commissioned to paint some frescoes in the Eremitani Church in Padua (above). By 1456 he had completed a series of scenes from the lives of Saint Christopher and Saint James. In 1944 the church suffered a direct bomb-hit and these key works of Mantegna's early style were destroyed. Efforts to patch them together, virtually flake by flake, have produced ghosts that only emphasize the magnitude of the loss. Earlier photographs exist (at right and below), but they can do little to suggest the over-all effect, where various scenes were unified by an elaborate inter-locking of perspective and foreshortening.

OPPOSITE: *Francesco Gonzaga, kneeling at the left, commissioned the* Madonna of Victory *for a new chapel in Mantua to celebrate his defeat of the French at Fornovo on July 6, 1495. On the first anniversary of the battle the painting was carried in procession and installed in the chapel. But the final victory went to the French after all: in 1797 the painting was brought to Paris by the French army, and it has remained there, in the Louvre, ever since.*

ment and fluidity on one hand, and of softened, sweetened, and gentled forms on the other, was a rejection necessary to the almost fanatic discipline that accounts for the intensity of the emotion he expresses. They find him cold. Yet in Mantegna, emotion is not so much held in check as it is distilled to an essence so pure that it is too strong for most palates. He is in many ways the most abstract, and hence the most modern, of all early Italian Renaissance painters. His special uses of perspective as an expressive device exemplify this fact.

Perspective is defined in the dictionary as "the art of picturing objects or a scene in such a way as to show them as they appear to the eye with reference to relative distance and depth." True enough, but the fascination of perspective is that it is based on a contradiction: it is a process of systematic distortion that, paradoxically, is a means toward the realistic representation of the world. Lines that are parallel in fact are inclined toward one another in perspective drawing; they converge. Large objects are made small, and small objects made large to express their distance from the eye. A disc becomes an oval to show that it is turned away from the observer. Squares become trapezoids. All objects are warped into false shapes in order to create the illusion of their true ones.

Since the camera does all this automatically, and since artists have been doing it for five hundred years, we forget the excitement of the fifteenth century when the rules for this distortion were being discovered. The creation of illusions of space, volume, and distance was a cross between a magician's trick and a scientific diagram, and it carried an impact that is so lessened for us today, through familiarity, that we must make an effort to imagine the preoccupation, to the point of obsession, of early Renaissance artists with this new device.

Perspective was a sudden enlargement of the artist's field

of expression; in virtually a literal way it opened new vistas. Before the perfection of perspective drawing, it was as if painters had had to stage their dramas on the apron—the part of the stage in front of the curtain—or at best in an extremely shallow space. Perspective raised the curtain and gave them not only all the stage but all the world behind it, to the deepest horizons. The rules for perspective could even be used in the fabrication of convincing vistas, heavenly or hellish, that the eye had never seen. The resultant art was not necessarily "better," since great art again and again is produced under limitations, but the means became more flexible and the potential range of expression wider, for any artist capable of making the most of them.

Mantegna made the most of perspective by conceiving his dramas in a full three dimensions—whether the space he was creating was limited to the bowered niche that embraces the figures of the *Madonna of Victory* (see page 75), or was extended as in the craggy and stony world of *The Agony in the Garden* (see pages 82–83). But these uses are usual, if expert. What distinguishes Mantegna in his use of perspective is that, more than any other artist of his time, he capitalized on it not as a form of realism but as a form of distortion that could intensify the emotional content of a painting.

In his earliest major work, the frescoes of the Eremitani Church in Padua (see page 74), Mantegna seems to have set out, with a prodigy's bravado, to demonstrate his mastery of perspective in a series of representations of saintly martyrdoms. By perspective he opened the wall in a series of cubicles filled with monumental structures and crowds of figures, but instead of conceiving each cubicle as if seen from a conventional level, he sharpened the perspective in the "cubicles" to make the scene take place well above the observer's position on the floor (see *Saint James Led to Martyrdom*, at the top of page 74). The effect of this device was not so much one of illusion as magical intensification of

the actors; and in a subject of potential violence, the only violence was supplied by a perspective that was in itself violent in the angles of its lines and its sudden juxtaposition of large and small figures (in the picture at lower right on page 74, compare the central figure with the small one holding a shield). What might have been only an ordinary representation of a *tableau vivant* becomes extraordinary in its air of threat and irreality.

To what extent this effect was precalculated is anybody's problem for discussion. But the principle revealed here was later employed by Mantegna in one of the most arresting paintings of his century, *Dead Christ* (see page 85). It is a picture impossible to pass by, a picture that jolts you with its first impression of violence. Yet by any objective analysis it is much more restrained than many paintings that, while they make a point of agony, carry none of the emotional shock of this one—a shock that Mantegna produces through the distortions involved in acute foreshortening. The height of the figure is so compressed that it is almost exactly equal to its width.

Many observers and some critics reject the picture in its Christian context; they admit its power as a representation of a corpse but find it only a disturbing reminder of the body's mortality impossible to associate with the idea of resurrection. This is a matter of individual response; the picture has always seemed to this observer as reverent as it is reserved. It is also a superb technical achievement in which Mantegna as a great craftsman comes out triumphant over the hazards presented by the daring concept of Mantegna the artist. The depiction of a human being lying down with the soles of his feet facing us could easily be ludicrous; it is, in fact, a standard gag shot with amateur photographers. But Mantegna proportioned the resultant distortions not by the laws of optics but by a combination of observation and discretion, creating an image that forces us into a new consciousness of the subject. It is as if we had

Inspired by the bas-reliefs on Roman monuments, Mantegna's Triumph of Caesar *(left) is a display of the paraphernalia of war and victory painted in sculpturesque terms. Denying the fluidity and suggestion of painting, Mantegna drew his* Judith *(opposite) in sepia with a cameo-carver's passion for absolute definition. Judith's profile is modeled as if it were intended for a Roman coin, and all forms are compressed into a limited space. Even the fluttering ribbon might well have been shaped with a chisel instead of drawn with a pen and brush.*

ANDREAS MANTEGNA·MCCCCLXXXXI · FEBR·

never before seen a representation of the dead Christ. The picture is powerful, moving, and true, where it might have been only eccentric.

Mantegna is never eccentric, but he is always original. His creation of an ancient classical world—which passed in his time for a sort of archaeological study—was an extraordinary piece of romantic invention; it is so convincing that it persists today as part of a picture we have reconstructed with an accuracy that contradicts Mantegna's vision. Obsessed by what he thought was the sculpture of antiquity, Mantegna himself probably considered his re-creations as a kind of archaeology, and in fact he was as close to being a scholar of the antique as was possible in his time. He was a collector and apparently to some extent a dealer in classical fragments, but his century knew classical sculpture only in bits and pieces, most of them miserably debased in style. Greek sculpture was only a legend; although the Parthenon was not yet a ruin, and its sculpture was nearly intact on its pediments, it was unknown in the West. The Roman sculpture that now lines the halls of our museums had only begun to be discovered.

To realize the originality of Mantegna's classical invention, we must remember that the predominantly classical architectural aspect of Italian cities that we now take for granted was not their aspect in Mantegna's time. Instead of cities filled with the adapted classical elements of baroque architecture and the later rejuvenated (or embalmed) neoclassic structures, Mantegna first knew cities where the architectural flavor remained medieval. During his lifetime the classical transformation was taking place, but it took place as modernism, and Mantegna's art contributed to the character it assumed.

From fragments, from forgeries, from literary references, probably from collections of drawings that artists passed around among themselves as sorts of pattern books, and from the wonderfully evocative but decayed and half-buried architectural stage-set of the ruins of ancient Rome itself, Mantegna distilled his own ancient world—a world of wonderful completeness and of an austere purity. In this curious way he became one of the mightiest Romans of them all.

Through the legerdemain of his immaculate craftsmanship as a painter he also became, in effect, one of the most inventive of early Renaissance architects and one of the most decorative sculptors. The architectural settings that serve as backgrounds for the martyrdoms in the Eremitani

frescoes may be buildings that were never planned to be built, but they would have been possible to build and are some of the most impressive architectural designs of their time on the classical model. In the background of the Louvre's *Saint Sebastian* (see page 86) Mantegna pictures a group of ruined buildings that give the event, nominally, a setting in the ancient world, but they are actually brilliant Renaissance designs first created and then shattered, a tour de force combining the vigorous genius of a Renaissance architect with the romantic nostalgia that accompanied the rebirth of classicism from the start.

As a sculptor-architect working in paint, Mantegna created, in the staggeringly illusionist ceiling of the Camera degli Sposi, some of his century's most beautiful bas-reliefs in an architectural framework. He seems to have taken delight in putting himself in the position of a sculptor forced to work in acutely limited depth, and of a painter forced to create his stone with his brush. The resultant hybrids, including such drawings as *Judith* (see page 77) and most directly the frieze of the *Triumph of Caesar,* combine the beauties of both parents in a new harmony.

The *Triumph of Caesar* (see page 76), perhaps inspired by the reliefs of the Arch of Titus, makes the most direct

Minerva Expelling the Vices from the Grove of Virtue (opposite) and a companion allegory called, perhaps inaccurately, Parnassus *(above) were painted by the aging Mantegna for young Isabella d'Este. Hybrids created by the old man's powerful style and the young woman's too-precious subject matter, they are the artist's most puzzling works.* Parnassus *shows Mars and Venus triumphant while Vulcan, Venus's wronged husband, rages in his cave (detail below), but the precise meaning is disputed by scholars.*

kind of reference to the classical past and expresses the spirit of military theatricality so often reflected in Mantegna's idea of the ancient world. There is no ambiguity in either the intention or the result—in contrast to Mantegna's two most puzzling paintings where, instead of re-creating a spectacle as it could have existed, he enters the field of lyrical allegory as a favor to a lady, Isabella d'Este.

Poor Isabella! She was a woman of considerable beauty and intellectual cultivation, but her misadventures with her "studio" in the Gonzaga palace have left her forever tainted with a bit of the flavor of a pretentious little bluestocking. At the age of sixteen she married Francesco Gonzaga, and as the new great lady of a small court she took over its cultural direction a little prematurely. Her studio, in competition with a similar project of her brother, Alfonso d'Este, grew into a combination of salon, retreat, art gallery, and flattering background intended as an apotheosis of the humanistic spirit. Isabella planned that the walls should be lined with a set of appropriate paintings by leading artists, and set about with youthful highhandedness to dictate to them. The great Bellini of Venice drily let her know that he regarded himself as more experienced and competent than she, but Mantegna, as the Gonzagas' court artist, was more indulgent. Meeting her at least halfway, he completed two paintings—*Minerva Expelling the Vices from the Grove of Virtue* and *Parnassus,* both now in the Louvre—along with such other paintings as were completed for the studio. Nobody, it appears, will ever know exactly who made what concessions to whom, or precisely what Mantegna had in mind in the so-called *Parnassus.* There have even been suggestions that Mantegna, now in his sixties, might have been very gently pulling his young patroness's leg—a thoroughly unlikely possibility since contemporary accounts reveal him as a severe and even acerbic personality.

Such a personality was not perfectly adaptable to the requirements of ornamenting a salon in an appropriately feminine character, but Mantegna sufficiently modified his manner to create a pair of pictures where sensuous opulence, ornamental elegance, and his own unrelenting formal disciplines are combined into a somewhat uneasy emulsion. *Minerva Expelling the Vices from the Grove of Virtue* (see page 78) presents no great problems of interpretation since its content is entirely expected from the explanatory title, and any figures that might offer problems are conveniently labeled. In a justifiable tendency to give Mantegna credit for all the good and leave Isabella responsible for any shortcomings in this May–December joint project, we can imagine her laying out the allegory, enumerating the vices and virtues on her fingers like a governess before a small boy, and Mantegna tolerantly going ahead to create a tableau where the final effect of fantasy is strong enough to hold its own against the rather elementary didactic allegory.

But the *Parnassus* (see page 79) bears no labels, and while there is not much question as to the identities of the Olympian figures involved, just what they are doing, and in what spirit they are doing it, is less certain. Apollo (just possibly Orpheus) is seated at the far left. The Muses dance in the center. Mercury, with a tamed and most wonderfully bizarre Pegasus, is at the far right, while Mars and Venus surmount the composition. Vulcan, Venus's blacksmith husband, is in a cave with his forge at the left, and is the object of attention by a cupid who blows in his direction through a long trumpet.

All of this, even more than its companion painting, suggests a stage and a pageant. In all probability it resembles the sets, gone without record, that Mantegna as part of his duties designed for the elaborate performances that were staged at court. But what goes on? Is the illicit love of Mars and Venus being celebrated here in an ennobled way, or is the whole thing, as some scholars believe, an exercise in the mock-heroic? Is there a half-humorous reason for

TEXT CONTINUED ON PAGE 89

LOUVRE

This majestic Crucifixion *(left), serene but intense, is one of three panels painted for the predella, or base, of an altarpiece in the church of San Zeno, Verona. The violence beneath its reserve is evident in the detail (opposite) of the soldiers casting lots for Jesus' robe. The altarpiece was carried off to France by Napoleon in 1797, and returned in 1815 minus the best part of it—the predella panels.*

OVERLEAF: *Detail by detail,* The Agony in the Garden *(another predella panel from San Zeno) may seem to offer little that is not found in the work of Mantegna's contemporaries: the disciples asleep, the file of centurions, the imagined Jerusalem on a rocky hill, the blasted tree. But what makes it unmistakably Mantegna's is its strangely compelling amalgam of the sinister and the mysterious.*

ON THE FOLLOWING PAGES: A PORTFOLIO IN GRAVURE OF PAINTINGS BY ANDREA MANTEGNA

BELOW: *The foreshortening in* The Dead Christ, *Mantegna's most audacious painting, is so extreme that it risks being ludicrous—and would be, if it had not produced an image so arresting that it forces a new consciousness of a standard subject. There is an earlier version of this picture without the two mourners, Saint John and the Virgin, who have been awkwardly crowded in at the left as the painting's one concession to convention. But even their intrusion cannot much reduce the atmosphere of majestic and tragic isolation that shocks us with its proclamation of our own mortality.*

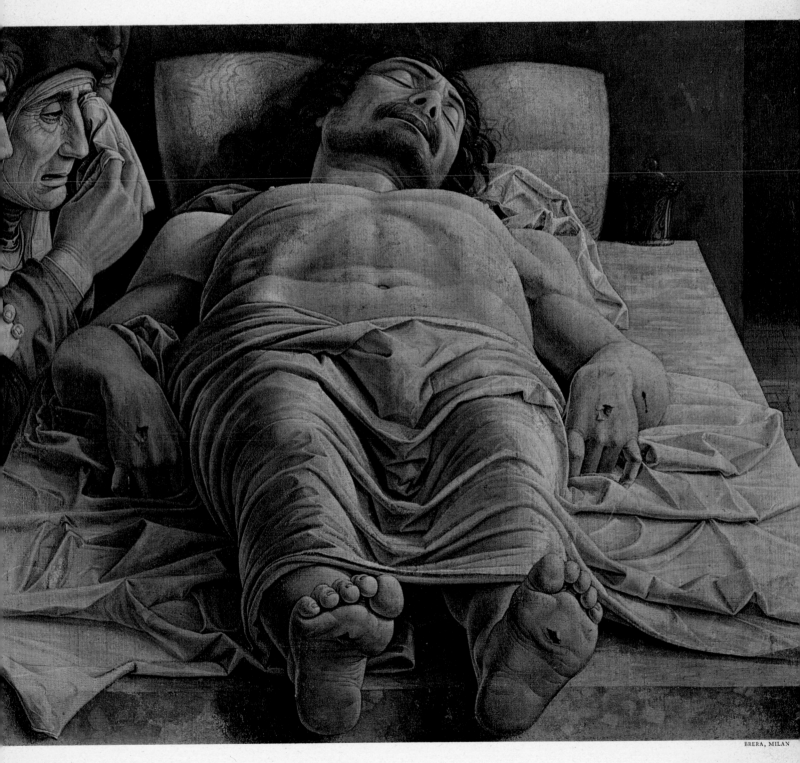

OPPOSITE: *In* The Presentation in the Temple *Mantegna pushes illusionism about as far as it will go, virtually assuming the roles of architect, goldsmith, and lapidary in the creation of delicately wrought and highly polished details. The painted bas-reliefs in the lunettes represent Abraham's sacrifice and Moses with the tablets of the Law.*

Saint Sebastian *(opposite), probably painted between 1475–80, shows Mantegna's mastery of the fantastic and the terrible in such details as the distant landscape (below) and the head of the executioner with his bow and quiver (above), as well as his ability to describe a gruesome martyrdom with paradoxical decorative elegance. The Roman setting of so much of the early history of the Christian church enabled Mantegna to combine his passion for antiquity with the subject matter dictated by commissions for religious paintings. Among these subjects Saint Sebastian was always a favorite; he is usually shown undraped and severely, though not mortally, wounded by arrows (after being left for dead he was rescued by a devout woman, recovered, and was then beaten to death with rods).*

TEXT CONTINUED FROM PAGE 80

making Mars an almost lissome matinee-idol type, a youthful philanderer, instead of showing him in his more conventional aspect as a mature, heavily muscled, hypermasculine man? Is the long horn blown by the cupid a "horn of fame" (it is of a type so used elsewhere), and is the fame thus visited upon Vulcan his unwelcome notoriety as cuckold? Above all, the two Muses at far right and, less noticeably, the two at far left have joined thumbs and fingers in a gesture still used in Italy as a bawdy reference to sexual union.

But the basic interpretation of art must be subjective, and this mock-heroic structure is denied by the picture's total effect of celebration rather than of levity. The love of Venus and Mars can also be interpreted sympathetically. For the Romans (and hence for Renaissance humanists) Mars was not only the god of war but the symbol of all that was brave, invincible, and glorious, while Venus was the goddess of spiritual as well as sensual love, the symbol of the beauty of the arts as well as the allure of the flesh. Under these identifications, Vulcan, who never manages to come out well, could symbolize the insensitive objector to an ideal union, and the cupid could be silencing his complaints.

For the observer aware of both possibilities, *Parnassus* slides maddeningly back and forth between them, never quite reaching fulfillment in either direction and seeming to shift to the contradictory attitude just as it is about to confirm one or the other. We are left with the conclusion, which can be reached only by assumption, that the disharmony between what Isabella wanted and what Mantegna would have chosen to do independently (although independently he would probably have chosen neither of the subjects of these two pictures for treatment of any kind) accounts for an ambiguous statement by an artist elsewhere remarkable for his certainty and clarity.

But if Mantegna's heart was not given over to the subject matter of Isabella's paintings, he gave her full value in their execution. Both paintings are rich visual experiences. Filled with glowing crags, shimmering fabrics, glittering jewels and metals, dense clusters of foliage studded with fruits, they are summaries of Mantegna's decorative vocabulary.

For Mantegna is, by the very least judgment, an unexcelled master of pure ornament, of art as pure delectation. But his genius was that he transformed a merely decorative vocabulary into an expressive one. The majority of his decorative elements are shared with other northern Italian painters, and he must have learned them, essentially from a style book, as an apprentice in Squarcione's workshop. Other apprentices emerged from the same shop with a style based on meaningless complications of drapery; on many repetitiously patterned swags and garlands of foliage, ribbons, and fruit; on tinny figures posed in attitudes of affected passion or nicety. But Mantegna took this improbable material, this set of mannered tricks, and transmuted it into a vocabulary of expressive power.

In great art there is always a residual inexplicable quality that accounts for greatness after all explanations are made. How to explain why Mantegna is not a monotonous painter? He should be. His decorative vocabulary is not large, and he only varies it from picture to picture. There is not much difference in texture between the striated boulders that jut from Mantegna's landscapes and the corded bodies of his martyred saints. A fluttering ribbon or a crumpled banner blowing from a bronze staff borne by a triumphant warrior may be as rigid as the staff itself. The stems of Mantegna's plants and the trunks of his trees rise from the rocky ground and spray outward in patterns electric with force, but they are immobile and their clusters of leaves and fruit are attached to them like enameled metal. No breeze can stir them in a world where even objects designated as being in motion are held quite still within the general enchantment.

It is this quality of enchantment that transforms what might just as well have been, but inexplicably is not, a mere studied desiccation. And it is this enchantment, this creation of an unreal world in which each detail is defined and incorporated into an indissoluble whole, that makes Mantegna a great religious painter and even a mystical one, although no accounts of him give us any reason to believe that in his day-to-day life he was anything but a practical, hardworking man.

Mantegna tells of the Crucifixion, or of the agony in the garden, or of any other episode in the Christian story, without comment and without personal interpretation. As a narrator he simply presents the story as everybody already knows it, and displays the participants with exceptional reserve. But this emotional understatement intensifies the power of the total picture; the emotion of the protagonists infuses every object within the painted scheme. No single element, not the smallest pebble, seems auxiliary; nothing is accidental, nothing can be thought of as temporary or reducible. Every object is charged with the full intensity of the total scene, and all is transfixed forever within the miracle.

No artist presents more bafflingly than Mantegna the puzzle of the creative process. Among all artists he is one of the last to whom the word "inspired" could ever be applied, yet of all artists he is one of the least mundane. But if he gives no answer to the puzzle, he at least makes the question irrelevant by his intensity and his completeness. Beyond a certain point great art is best accepted, like miracles, without explanation.

This is the second of a series of HORIZON *articles about great artists by John Canaday, art critic of* The New York Times. *In the next issue he will discuss the sixteenth-century German master Albrecht Dürer.*

For further reading: Mantegna: Paintings, Drawings, Engravings *by E. Tietze-Conrat (Phaidon—New York Graphic, 1955); "Andrea Mantegna" by Sir Kenneth Clark, a lecture in* Journal of the Royal Society of Arts, *August, 1958;* Mantegna *by Giuseppe Fiocco (Abrams, 1963); "The Education of Renaissance Man" by Iris Origo,* HORIZON, *January, 1960.*

This small Madonna and Child *(11⅜″ x 8½″) is one of Mantegna's most tender and intimate paintings. In adapting his sometimes hard-bitten style to gentler uses, as here, he did not sentimentalize: Mother and Child remain figures of spiritual regality.*

surrounded Barnes approach would appear to be made up of banalities. Perhaps in the twenties, when the memory of the Armory Show still aroused passions, these ideas were not so naïve and banal. It may be that time has simply caught up with and overtaken the Barnes Foundation.

When Barnes was questioned as to whether or not the gallery was open to the public, he said, "The general public is admitted if it conforms to the conditions of the educational institution." The wily Barnes was once more trying to confuse the so-called educational program with admission to the art gallery. It was a gambit which the Foundation and its trustees attempted again and again in order to obscure the facts.

The trustees admitted that the art gallery was physically in use for lectures to students only twelve hours a week, nine months a year. Figuring a six-hour day and a six-day week, which is customary for most museums, this left twenty-four hours during the week when the public might make use of the gallery without disturbing the lectures.

At the very time that hundreds of people were phoning or writing to me to complain that they could not gain admission to the art gallery, the trustees continued to insist that it was open to the public. On this question one could easily join issue and prove simple facts. If the public could see the collection of paintings under reasonable conditions, I believed that the state would have done its duty, whatever the merits of the educational program. Principles of free speech certainly require that the Foundation be at liberty to propagate any ideas short of sedition.

Since no lectures had been scheduled on Friday, Saturday, or Sunday for the past decade or longer, I suggested to counsel for the Foundation that the gallery be open to the public at least on those days. This was met with a flat refusal. The reason: on occasion, very irregularly, Miss De Mazia might give an additional lecture on Fridays. Hence the gallery must be kept empty every Friday so that she could feel free to give this lecture when the spirit moved her. And Saturday? On Saturdays the faculty (all four of them) met and planned the week's work; i.e., one lecture each. The public could not be permitted to intrude when these four individuals were in the gallery. The fact that there are several conference rooms in the building was brushed aside as immaterial. And Sunday? Mrs. Barnes lives, rent-free, in a large house (also tax-exempt) in the same grounds, and did not care to be disturbed by having "the public" on the premises on Sunday.

The narrow issue before the Supreme Court of Pennsylvania was whether the state had a right to make any inquiry into the operations of a charitable foundation; more specifically, whether the Barnes Foundation and the trustees had to file an answer or whether the Complaint should be dismissed. The Court, on March 22, 1961, held that the Complaint stated a good cause of action and ruled that: "The Attorney General of this Commonwealth not only has the authority but the duty to ascertain what are the facts surrounding the school in the Foundation to determine if it should be insu-

lated from the shock of taxation which hits all other citizens and enterprises in the land." The Court sent the case back to the trial judge and ordered the Foundation to answer the Complaint. But it did not stop there. Justice Michael A. Musmanno, speaking for a unanimous court, declared: "If the Barnes art gallery is to be open only to a selected, restricted few, it is not a public institution; and if it is not a public institution, the Foundation is not entitled to tax exemption as a public charity. This proposition is incontestable."

Nonetheless, the Barnes Foundation more than two years later had not accepted it. Certain friends of the Foundation, including lawyers who should know better, suggested that the Foundation pay real property taxes, drop its claim of tax exemption, and continue to exclude the public. But a foundation cannot legally change its status at the whim of the trustees. Once property is dedicated irrevocably to charitable use, it cannot be reclaimed for private use. The purposes may be modified with the approval of the court; the institution may cease; but the property remains subject to the jurisdiction of the court to be applied to a similar charitable purpose. As a practical matter, even if the Foundation could renounce its charitable function, its ten million dollars of liquid assets would be insufficient to pay the taxes and penalties which might theoretically have been due since its establishment in 1922. In these four decades no property taxes have been paid on its choice acreage on the Philadelphia Main Line, or on the handsome residence occupied by Dr. and Mrs. Barnes. No taxes have been paid on the Barnes country estate in Chester County known as Ker Feal, where part of the Barnes arboretum is located. (Incidentally, although botanists occasionally visit the arboretum there, the general public has never been admitted to Ker Feal, and the state has been unable to find out what, if any, art works it contains.) No income tax has been paid on stock dividends or capital gains or gift tax on the Barnes Company stock transferred to the Foundation. No personal property tax on the collection has ever been paid. No gift tax was paid on the collection of paintings transferred by Barnes to the Foundation. No inheritance tax on the property or the paintings was paid on the death of Barnes. It has been estimated that the total taxes without penalties would have been in excess of thirty million dollars if all of these transactions had been taxable.

Immediately after the Supreme Court decision, and pending a final outcome of the case in the trial court, the Foundation quietly instituted a program admitting twenty-five visitors for two hours a day twice each week. The time limit allowed the visitor slightly more than seven seconds per picture, excluding artifacts and time to walk from room to room. Obviously the state could not consider that such a plan complied with the court's decree.

After all sorts of delay the trial judge finally acceded to the state's request for information from the Foundation. I then moved to have the Foundation furnish answers to a number of questions. I wanted to know how much money the Foundation had; I demanded an inventory of the collection, and an appraisal; also, a list of persons who had applied for admission, and a list of those who had actually been admitted. In addition, I wanted a list of the employees, the floor plan of the museum, and permission to have three experts visit the gallery to advise the court on the optimum number of visitors who could be admitted to the gallery at any one time. (The Foundation maintained that the gallery could not accommodate more than twenty-five people despite the fact that more than seventy persons attended Miss De Mazia's lectures.)

The Foundation asserted that its finances were none of the state's business, and declared that it did not have an inventory of the works of art. But finally, after a court order, it made available to the state a heterogeneous jumble of unfiled papers. Included in this welter was a little guest book of the type that can be found in a five-and-dime store. This was, in fact, the visitors' register of the multimillion-dollar Foundation for the years 1956 and 1957. It disclosed that the total number of people admitted to the gallery in 1956 was 326; the total number of visitors admitted in 1957 was 373. In 1956 visitors were present in the gallery on forty-four days; in 1957 visitors were admitted on only forty-one days.

Also among the papers were hundreds of requests for admission. I recognized some of the applicants as officials of the United Nations and of various foreign governments. Other letters were written on the stationery of renowned museums and universities. The carbon copies of the replies were also included. In nearly every instance the response to these courteous, sometimes fawning pleas was over the signature of Miss De Mazia, and informed the hapless applicant that the Barnes Foundation was not a "public gallery" and that the press of the educational activities prevented the admission of visitors. One exception was made in the case of Lessing Rosenwald, owner of a superb collection of prints. He was at first refused, but later, through the intercession of his gardener with Mrs. Barnes's gardener, received an invitation to visit the gallery.

Who were the favored few permitted to enter the sacred portals? The figures quoted do not account for repeat visitors, and a number came several times each year. These were almost invariably former students of the Foundation. The big visiting day each year was the day on which the spouses of the students were admitted to the holy of holies.

The Foundation, on order of the court, furnished the architectural plans of the gallery. It is an impressive two-story limestone building that provides twenty-three picture galleries, the largest 22 feet 10 inches by 26 feet 10 inches.

Having made this information available to the state, the Barnes Foundation capitulated. On December 12, 1960, almost two years after the filing of the action, a consent decree was entered. The Barnes Foundation agreed, and the court entered an order requiring the public to be admitted to the gallery on Friday and Saturday each week except during July and August. Two hundred persons were to be admitted on each visiting day: one hundred by prior arrangement, strictly in the order in which requests were received, and the other hundred on a first-come basis. Art students and teachers of art were to be admitted by special arrangement. A telephone, for handling inquiries, was to be installed for the first time.

The resourcefulness of the Foundation in keeping its doors closed to the general public continued unabated. Nearly three months went by. On March 18, 1961, all excuses having been exhausted, the gallery was opened; then the Foundation suddenly discovered a local fire ordinance prohibiting more than three people on the second floor at any one time. It was many months and more litigation before the Barnes Foundation erected a fire escape. Meantime, frustrated art lovers got no farther than the first floor.

The visitors who queued up as early as 7:30 A.M. for admission at 9:30 did not find their long wait uneventful. They were accosted by an array of pickets who passed out literature charging that the state was destroying education. Many of these vociferous people were, or had been, students in Miss De Mazia's course. They wrote to the Governor, to candidates for political office, to the newspapers. The husband of one of them wrote a book, the publication of which was subsidized by former Barnes students. And day after day they annoyed the visitors.

Finally, the iron gates would be opened by a platoon of Pinkerton detectives. Even today, paying a visit to the Barnes Foundation is like finding oneself in a Kafka play. The uniformed, stony-faced attendant opens the huge iron gate. The people wait and wait. The magic number of 100 is counted off, and the gates are slammed shut. Since very few remain until closing time, 4:30 in the afternoon, the gallery is practically empty most of the afternoon, except for the Pinkerton guards. Yet, as many as seventy-one people have been turned away in a single day. Occasionally number 101 or 102 is a foreigner who rails in disgust at American democracy. Not long ago Professor Igor N. Diakanoff of the University of Leningrad, who was visiting Philadelphia as a guest of the United States Government, declared on the basis of his experience at the Barnes Foundation that America is a police state.

After being permitted by the Pinkerton guard to enter the gate, the visitor is warned not to step on the grass and not to loiter. Inside the gate another Pinkerton detective sits comfortably in an automobile as, gimlet-eyed, he watches the visitors through the car window. It is a long walk from the street to the gallery. At the entrance to the building there is another Pinkerton detective. Two attendants check the coats and put the ladies' pocketbooks in a locker. The dime for the locker is returned to the lady when she retrieves her pocketbook. There are twenty-seven guards in the twenty-three rooms of the gallery. In addition, there is Miss De Mazia, who is in constant attendance either as the gracious chatelaine receiving the homage of the visiting serfs or as a twenty-eighth detective keeping under constant surveillance any artists, critics, or scholars she suspects to be unfriendly.

The lighting is dim. There is no catalogue. The pictures are not identified by name or number. The guards are totally uninformed, and the visitor seeks in vain the title of the picture he is looking at. Small metal plates with the name of the artist are affixed to the picture frames, but since many paintings are hung at least ten feet above the floor, only the far-sighted can make out the dingy plates.

Many pictures, however, are so famous as to be startling. In the main gallery alone, there are three murals by Matisse in the lunettes above the French doors, as well as Cézanne's *Woman with the Green Hat* and several Renoirs. Casually interspersed among the moderns, there are works by Titian, El Greco, and Hieronymus Bosch, not to mention an entry or two by Violette de Mazia and by Albert Nulty, a former trustee and chauffeur of Barnes. The common people are represented among the artists even if not welcomed as visitors.

On June 28, 1961, the trustees of the Barnes Foundation, without seeking court permission, voted to impose a two-dollar admission charge. The reason given was that operation costs were so high that the Foundation would be operating in the red unless it had additional income. A temporary injunction restraining the imposition of the charge was immediately obtained by the state, which then sued to enforce the consent decree.

Although this was the fourth time the Foundation had been brought to court, it was the first time that a full-scale hearing on the actual operation of the Foundation had ever been held, and a most extraordinary story unfolded. All five trustees testified and were asked how they qualified for their positions. This was an important point, since the court has the power and the duty to remove incompetent trustees in order to preserve the charity in the public interest. The brochure put out by the Foundation states:

Appreciation of works of art requires organized effort and systematic study, on the same principle that it requires effort and study to become a lawyer, an engineer, or a physician.

One would assume that, in accordance with this philosophy, the trustees—who have control of more than ten million dollars cash assets, valuable land and buildings, and the priceless collection of art, and are entrusted with operating an educational program both in art appreciation and in botany—would need to be singularly well qualified. But what sort of trustees did Barnes himself approve? Here, as elsewhere, Barnes had his own ideas.

The first trustee called was Nelle E. Mullen. A stolid, white-haired woman, Miss Mullen sat in the witness chair phlegmatically, and only occasionally deigned to reply to a direct question. She represents, perhaps, Barnes's prime effort at education of what he called "the rabble." Nelle E. Mullen has been employed either by the Barnes business or the Foundation since 1902. She has had no formal education beyond grade school. She has had no special training in business, finance, or the management of an art gallery. But, when

Dr. Albert C. Barnes
Founder of the Barnes Foundation

the Foundation was ordered to admit the public to the art gallery, she did not consult anyone outside it about hiring guards or making the other necessary arrangements, believing, as she put it, that she knew best.

The next trustee to appear was Sidney Frick, the son of the Foundation's lawyer, and himself an attorney. He had had no training in art or in the management of a museum. "I have attended the Guggenheim Museum in New York on two occasions," said he. "I have been to the Metropolitan Museum in New York on one occasion. I visited the museums. I did not consult the directors."

Next came Joe Langran, a landscape architect who lectures at the Barnes Foundation and receives a salary. He testified frankly that until the hearing he was unaware of the limited backgrounds of his fellow trustees. He himself has had no training in museum management, finance, or related subjects.

The focal figure of the litigation was Miss De Mazia, for it was she who wrote the bulk of the letters refusing admittance to the gallery. Everything about this woman was shrouded in mystery; even her true name was in doubt. In an earlier case she testified under oath and gave her name as Yetta de Mazia. She signs her name Violette de Mazia in all correspondence, and this was the name she gave when called to the witness stand this time. She testified that she first came to the United States in 1927, and that she had attended schools in France and Belgium. Since her arrival in the United States she has had no education in art or any other subject except at the Barnes Foundation. She has had no training or experience elsewhere in museum management. She did not consult any museum directors or qualified persons with respect to managing the Barnes Foundation gallery.

Her testimony with respect to her education prior to coming to the United States appears to be lacking in candor. For example:

Q. I think the last question was: Where did you go to school?
A. In London and then at the Barnes Foundation.
Q. What was the name of the art school in London?
A. The Hampstead Conservatoire and the Camden Art School, and the Polytechnic School.
Q. Do you have any degrees from those institutions?
A. No. They are not institutions that gave degrees.

On recross-examination she was confronted with a letter from the Polytechnic School stating that there was no record that she had ever attended the institution.

MRS. FORER: I will ask leave of Court to hold the record open for a certificate from the Polytechnic Institute to the effect that they have never had Miss De Mazia as a student from the year 1880.

MISS DE MAZIA: I was not a student.

She was asked about the practice of the museum in refusing to co-operate with scholars. James Thrall Soby, for example, had requested and been denied permission to visit the gallery in 1953 when he was writing a book on Di Chirico. Henri Dorra, when he was with the Corcoran Gallery, sought in vain to get permission to photograph the Barnes Seurats. (He finally obtained admission to the gallery under an assumed name.) Alfred H. Barr, Jr., director of collections of The Museum of Modern Art, was refused permission to study or reproduce any of the Matisse paintings. The testimony of Miss De Mazia on this issue is as follows:

Q. Do you make available to art historians and art students engaged in research, reproductions and materials from The Barnes Gallery?
A. We do not sell reproductions.
Q. Do you make them available to use?
A. We don't have any.
Q. Do you make available to them any material?
A. Such as?
Q. Do you have any, such as an inventory of your collection?
THE COURT: A catalogue?
A. No.

Trustee Nelle E. Mullen, on the other hand, testified that the Foundation has a card index and a photograph of each item in the collection.

The fifth trustee is Barnes's widow, an active, alert lady in her late eighties. She still teaches at the arboretum and takes a real interest in its work. She testified voluntarily. Mrs. Barnes stated that she had a degree from the University of Pennsylvania, that she welcomes visitors to the arboretum, and that she sends specimens of plants to botanists all over the world. No complaint has ever been made to the state that the arboretum denies information or admission to scholars.

Even after the consent decree, however, the art gallery, under the guidance of Miss De Mazia, continued to put up all kinds of unreasonable obstacles to exclude scholars. Professor Millard Meiss, president of the International Committee of the History of Art and a member of the Institute for Advanced Study at Princeton, wrote to me on April 25, 1962, as follows:

For the first time in its century of existence the International Society [of the History of Art] held a meeting in the United States last fall. This meeting was attended by some sixty-five leading scholars from abroad. American scholars, who were for the first time acting as hosts to their foreign colleagues, had to hang their heads in shame because the Barnes Foundation refused to admit a group of scholars at any other hour than an impossible eight o'clock in the morning. The President of the society at that time, Professor Marcel Aubert, spent a half hour on the telephone in vain attempting to persuade the Foundation to be more hospitable.

When questioned about this extraordinary incident, Miss De Mazia stated that she could not remember such a telephone call or request to the Foundation.

The financial practices of the Foundation take the bewildered citizen into a wonderland where words have lost their common meanings. From the inception of the case in the spring of 1958, the state made every effort to get a financial report from the Foundation. The answer of the Barnes Foundation to this motion contained the following sworn statement:

Defendants (The Foundation and the trustees) deny that information with respect to funds for employment of additional personnel, making any changes in management operation in maintenance of the gallery, purchase of additional insurance and like matters is essential in this proceeding for any purpose. *There is no denial that sufficient funds are available for employment of any additional personnel or making changes in management operation in maintenance of the gallery, were any needed.* (Italics mine.)

In utter forgetfulness or disregard of this pleading, Trustee Frick testified under oath as follows:

Q. When you became aware of the fact that there appeared to be this operating shortage, although there was some $300,000 income, you were going to, perhaps run short, did you analyze the budget to determine what items could be reduced?
A. In the first place, we were aware that this was very likely to happen before this visitation program was embarked upon.

He further testified that knowing there would be a shortage of funds to meet payments for guards and clerical assistance, the trustees did nothing either to reduce expenses or to increase income. There is a specific prohibition in the trust indenture against paying salaries to trustees. Barnes provided, however, that some of the people he selected as trustees would be well paid for other "services" to the Foundation. Mrs. Barnes continues to receive a salary of $30,000 per annum for being President of the Foundation. Miss De Mazia gets a salary of $10,000 a year. Miss Mullen receives $12,000 for her clerical and bookkeeping services. No thought apparently has been given to charging the art students a fee, although there is nothing in the trust indenture which provides that there shall be free instruction (but the indenture does specify that the public shall be admitted "free" to the gallery).

Of the cash income of $305,076 which the Foundation receives annually on its investments, only 19.7 per cent is devoted to the operation and maintenance of the art gallery. Despite Barnes's specific provision that a director for the art gallery be employed at his death, this priceless collection has no professional director. Trustee Langran's explanation of the failure to employ a director is interesting:

Q. Do you think it the duty of a trustee who is himself not a professionally qualified person, to employ a professionally qualified expert in the operation of a multimillion-dollar enterprise?

A. Well, I think if we could afford it, it would be very desirable.

The most dubious practice in the care of the Barnes paintings was inadvertently revealed by Miss De Mazia. She was questioned about the discontinuance of her lecture series on the ostensible ground that the admission of the public to the gallery on Fridays interfered with her Tuesday lectures. She testified that she needed a few extra lectures and that these would have been held on Friday in addition to the regularly scheduled Tuesday lectures. This is her explanation:

Q. You could, of course, have scheduled your classes which you held every third—is it every third or fourth—

A. About. Irregular.

Q. Irregular? You could have scheduled them for some morning, could you not?

A. No, that is completely impossible, because, for each class—for instance—talking about my class on Tuesday afternoon—our attendant at the gallery starts to prepare—meaning gathering paintings in a certain room or rooms, rather rehanging others, bringing furniture that I might use for a particular talk. I am there on Tuesday morning quite early and go over and change, according to the light, or according to my last-minute, perhaps, thought . . . So, in the morning, we could not possibly have a class. *That takes place every morning of every class day.* (Italics mine.)

I was astounded to learn that these paintings, many of which are old and fragile, others of enormous size—and all irreplaceable—were regularly being shifted about four days a week. I promptly checked with museums and art authorities to find out if this practice was as unusual and deleterious as I thought.

Professor Hartt of the University of Pennsylvania testified that "Every time a work of art is moved, it inevitably shortens by somewhat the life of this work." The court was not impressed. The argument was made that these were

Miss Violette de Mazia
Lecturer at the Barnes Foundation

Barnes's paintings and this was what he wanted done. Whether or not he actually wanted the paintings moved about is highly questionable in view of the fact that he provided that the classes be held in his home after his wife's death and not in the art gallery. But more basic is the question of the right of trustees to jeopardize property entrusted to their care.

Charles Sterling, who is a curator of paintings at the Louvre, a full professor at New York University's Institute of Fine Arts, and foreign advisor to the National Gallery of Canada, was fortunately in New York at the time of the trial. After a tremendous legal battle, the state was permitted to take his deposition in New York. His testimony seemed to me to be unequivocal.

Q. Now, there has also been testimony that in connection with the so-called art classes conducted by the Foundation the pictures are moved around; they're taken from the wall and moved from one room to another every day for the lectures. Is this consonant with good museum practice?

PROF. STERLING: If you permit me to just say this is unusual, certainly, and what are the slides for? They have precisely been invented to avoid moving of the original pictures because—well, I wouldn't say that—it's absolutely evident that each moving of the picture damages the picture, but it can happen. If you move pictures very often, you multiply the chance of their being dropped, and if it is an old painting that it suffers enormously from being suddenly dropped, and that can happen.

We in the Louvre always avoid, and all museums avoid very carefully, moving around of pictures. For instance, the photographers always ask us to move the picture in different light and better light. We constantly refuse it because we rather prefer to have a special light, artificial light, put on the picture than to bring precious pictures to a, to the window and then put it back, you know, because in the moving [of pictures] there is always a danger, a potential danger.

When this evidence was offered, counsel for the Foundation contended that what Professor Sterling meant was that it is *not* evident that moving damages the pictures. And so the paintings continue to be moved, to this very day.

The extremes to which the guards will go in annoying visitors are well described by Professor Sterling:

And, I must say that the way the guards enforce their, the respect of the rules they have—for instance, when I was talking with somebody who was with me and I was talking to him I had a—the chief of the guards who followed me, by the way, from room to room, he shouted at me from the other part of the room that my hands were too close to the pictures, and he shouted in such a way that everybody stared at us—at me. Well, I don't find that normal procedure for a guard. Those are not guards, you see, but really policemen, and I had the feeling as if I were a convict from a jail who was permitted to go to the circus or something under the surveillance of wardens who permitted themselves to shout at you.

By their own words, I believe, the trustees showed their incompetence to manage the Foundation and their bad faith. Eight different provisions of the trust indenture creating the Foundation have not been carried out. In addition, the court decree provided that special arrangements be made for art students and teachers to view the collection. The Foundation has not done anything about this except to say it would be willing to make special provisions for art students and teachers to attend Miss De Mazia's classes. And to this date the Foundation has refused to file with the state an accounting of its funds and its property.

Far more important than the substantial sums of money involved, is the whereabouts of many important paintings. For example, Maurice Tuchman of the Guggenheim Museum staff wrote to inform me that in 1923 Barnes purchased more than one hundred paintings by Soutine. Only about a dozen are on exhibit. Where are the rest? Are they being properly stored? Similar questions arise in connection with many of the other works of art.

After careful consideration, and after consultation with many scholars, I concluded that the government would be derelict in its duty if it did not make every effort to change the management of the Foundation. At the close of the testimony, on behalf of the state, I made a motion to have four of the trustees removed. (Since Mrs. Barnes was qualified with respect to her management of the arboretum and since there had been no complaints of arrogant refusal of admission or co-operation, her removal was not sought.) The motion was denied. The two-dollar admission charge was reduced by the trial court to one dollar. The judge himself found that a proper investment of the ten million dollars would yield ample income for reasonable security measures (the trustees, however, prefer to invest more than seven of these millions in low-yield municipal securities).

The state has not appealed the decision. Meanwhile, the paintings may still be jeopardized, and the public is still harassed. Eventually time will compel the appointment of new trustees. But the prospect of getting a real change in management within the next ten years is not hopeful.

Barnes is only one of many foundations which exist by reason of the tax subsidy granted to charities by the local, state, and Federal governments. Many perpetuate the whims and caprices of their founders or trustees in utter disregard of the public policy that charities are to receive special privileges so that they may serve the good of the community. In some cases, rare manuscripts are locked up and kept away from scholars. In others, valuable letters and documents are destroyed by trustees whose ideas of morality and taste override the public interest. Hundreds if not thousands of institutions for the young, the handicapped, and the aged perpetuate racial discrimination and religious bigotry at the behest of some dead founder or arrogant trustee. To date the courts have been reluctant to inquire into the management of these charities and foundations, permitting the dead hand of the donor to exercise control from beyond the grave in defiance of law and common sense.

Much of the tacit ideological basis for the insulation of foundations not only from taxation but also from government regulation is predicated upon a distrust of the ordinary citizen. It is presumed that the donor by reason of his acquisition or inheritance of great wealth was endowed with superior wisdom and exceptional rights. Although the rest of us must conform to legal requirements and pay taxes, these favored few, like the Platonic guardians, need not account to society. Mrs. Barnes expressed the feeling succinctly. After graciously conducting me about the gallery for some three hours, she remarked, "Now that you have seen how wonderful this collection is, you can understand why we cannot have the public here."

Lois G. Forer has been practicing law in Pennsylvania for twenty-five years. She and her husband, who is also a lawyer, have three children and live in Germantown.

I SHALL NOT LOOK UPON HIS LIKE AGAIN

Hamlet, Act 1, Scene 2

A few exceptions, assembled by Max Brandel

Sumerian head, limestone and
lapis lazuli, c. 2500 B.C.
Nelson Gallery, Kansas City

Arnold Stang

Roman sepulchral relief,
marble, first century B.C.
Metropolitan Museum of Art

James Cagney

Egyptian magistrate,
black schist, c. 300 B.C.
Cairo Museum

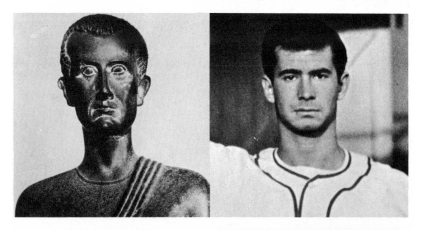

Tony Perkins

Roman head of Augustus,
marble, first century A.D.
Metropolitan Museum of Art

James Mason

Bette Davis

Roman head of Agrippina,
marble, first century A.D.
Louvre

Marlon Brando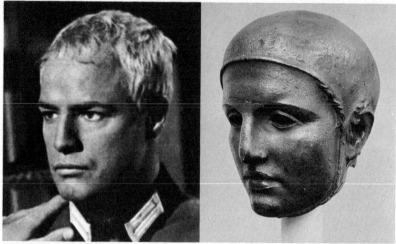

Head of a young priest,
Etruscan bronze, c. 200 B.C.
British Museum

Jerry Colonna

Greek head from high-relief
panel, after 570 B.C.
Acropolis Museum, Athens

Fernandel

Egyptian functionary,
wood, c. 2500 B.C.
Louvre

The Greek islands of the Aegean Sea are beautiful in a shapely, unwasteful way, nothing opulent anywhere, not an extra frill. They form linear, gray-blue shapes on the blazing summer sea, looking from a distance remote, unreal, and unworldly, like myths.

Space, silence, and emptiness were the elements of this Aegean world as we sailed into it early in June. It was as though some loudspeaker, after bawling in our ears for so long we were no longer conscious of it, had suddenly become still, and we were relieved more than had seemed possible.

Ahead of us in the sea appeared a boat, one. It came wallowing out of the blue haze toward us, a caïque, with high bow and stern, wide amidships, the mainsail at an angle, the hull painted a fresh and pretty blue striped with green. It was clearly going out of its way to pass close to us and our pilot shifted course too, to pass close to it. There was no reason for any recognition or exchange between the two ships but it was *lonely* out here, and each wanted a good look at the other, if only to see new human faces. The caïque, pitching a little, passed by quite near us; in the little cabin door the skipper eyed us intently and the cabin boy practically danced on deck as he waved. We waved and shouted back and then went on into the bluish solitude, toward the island of Hydra in the haze ahead.

We sailed along Hydra's forbidding cliff shoreline until we came to a natural bowl in the rock face, an amphitheatre curving back from the sea, with white houses climbing gradually and then steeply up toward the surrounding rock cliffs. It looked like the setting for some ideal musical comedy, and as we sailed into this little port at noon—past an old canon emplacement on the left and a sea wall on the right—a bell began to toll melodiously, as though on cue in the theatre. The sound came from a stone bell tower in the center of the port, and from the portal at the foot of the tower a procession slowly moved out into the sparkling sunlight. An acolyte holding a palm design on a long pole led the procession. After him came others holding medallions on long poles, then priests in white cassocks and black hats, and finally several men carrying a handsome and strangely happy-looking coffin.

Following that came a small crowd, including naval officers in white. This pageant moved along the colorful quay, turned into a little street between two lively cafés, and wound slowly up toward a piece of ground on a promontory above the port which was full of white mausoleums and of those prizes in Greece, trees, including a number of splendid cypresses.

As a funeral, it was a failure. The bell could only toll musically, the water danced in the snappy breeze, the white houses sparkled, the blue sky glowed, and the white cassocks flashed in the sunshine. Death itself looked happy on the Greek islands.

By two o'clock in the afternoon the wharf, or the agora—market—was deserted. Sailors slept in the shade of their caïques, a waiter in one of the small restaurants carefully put two tables together in the shade, laid himself out like a corpse on top of them, his hands folded on his chest, and fell asleep.

For some reason or other I set off across the empty shadeless cobblestones of the agora, the only thing moving there. The sunshine immediately came down so heavily on my head and shoulders that I was forced into a reverie, feeling forgetful and reflective but with nothing to forget and nothing to reflect on, the inside of my head becoming like a movie house that had been flooded with sunshine and so put out of operation. I ambled on over the cobbles,

The oracle is silent at Delphi,

and Delos has long been deserted,

but on the isles of Greece

life is still lived naturally and fully

In the LIGHT of the AEGEAN

By JOHN KNOWLES

wondering hazily how far it was to the shade of a wall at the other end of the agora, feeling content, slowly asking myself whether the sun hadn't drifted a little closer to the earth today than ever before and whether in a minute I might smell my hair beginning to smolder. That's the kind of sun it was. Eventually I made it to the strip of shade, and began to realize that the people of these islands spend three or four months every year under that implacable sun, and to appreciate the influence it must have on their lives.

Twelve weeks later, when I was again on Hydra, I saw a cloud, my first Greek cloud. It gathered its small white self together in the pure blueness of the sky, and in a lonely way sailed across the sky and off in the direction of Russia. Everybody stopped whatever they were doing to look wonderingly at it.

The sun was always there, all summer long, and nothing ever stood between it and the Aegean islands except occasionally a thin haze. The sun burned down strongly at seven in the morning, and was still pouring down at seven at night.

We had lunch at a café on the agora, at a plain wooden table on the marblelike paving stones. There was nothing fussy about the restaurant or about the food; there was nothing fussy, I learned as the summer wore on, about Greece.

A gust of wind suddenly plunged across the agora at us, driving the big canvas awning over the café wildly back and forth on its guide wires, and then drifting away again and leaving calmness behind. We went on eating. Abruptly another gust hurled itself at us; this time a waiter was standing next to the awning and he grabbed it. A moment later he found himself ten feet in the air. He swung there for a few moments while the Greeks roared with laughter, and then he fell swinging back to earth, breathing heavily but with a game grin.

The Aegean wind, turbulent as madness, was one of the fundamental facts of life on these islands. Work, going to sea, sleep, tem-

pers—all were deeply conditioned by it; it was as strong a force there as the sun itself.

After lunch I went to a pile of boulders near the port for a swim. Raw gusts of wind had whipped the sea into engulfing the lower rocks, where there were ladders for people to get in and out of the water. Today they would have to sweep up to a ladder on the crest of a wave, catch it, and pull themselves up before the heavy receding wave dragged them back across the rocks at the foot of the ladder. Most of the two dozen people on hand were therefore not going in; in fact, when I arrived there was only one bather, a large woman bobbing placidly enough from crest to foaming crest.

Eventually she decided to come out. I watched, we all watched, as she bobbed along toward the rocks and the ladder. She maneuvered herself to within about ten feet of them and started forward with a wave. But in her slowness she lost the wave, which swept up to the ladder ahead of her and then quickly receded, leaving a gulf that revealed the jagged rocks below, toward which she began to be rushed by the next rapidly approaching wave. Desperately flailing backward, the woman managed to avoid being dashed against the rocks by the full impact of the wave; she disappeared in a swirl of foam and then came bobbing and panting to the wind-swept surface again.

There were six young Greek men on the rocks; they reacted as though they were one. They catapulted into the sea in good and bad dives, and quickly all of them were around the distressed swimmer, supporting her and pulling and tugging and working her toward the rocks again. A wave rose up behind them all, and the group splashed and bobbed up to the rocks and ladder. Two of the Greeks were flung against the rocks, but the woman was shielded between them and two others fixed her hands at the right instant onto a rung of the ladder. As they, too, were scraped back across the rocks by the receding waves, she managed to pull herself to safety. Then the

young men, three of them bleeding from bruises, came out of the water themselves.

It was a brave exhibition, and when one of the rescuers sat down near me to dab his scraped leg with a towel I congratulated him. "Thank you," he said, smiling happily, "it was nothing." Reflecting on the nobility and stoicism of classical Greece, I thought this was a surviving streak of it. "Here four thousand of the Peloponnese once fought with three thousand thousand . . . Stranger, go tell the Spartans that we lie here obedient to their commands," read the famous memorial to the heroic dead at Thermopylae. That was the spirit.

We gathered again at dusk aboard the *Toscana*. Around us the natural amphitheatre of Hydra rose on three sides. All the life of the island was concentrated here; a dusty track or two trailed away from it for short distances along the sides of the cliff and then petered out. There were no vehicles of any kind on the island; donkeys were the only transportation. There was one telephone, at the post office. There was of course no television; there is none anywhere in Greece. There was "running water" in some houses, in a manner of speaking. It ran this way. A boat would arrive in the port at unstated intervals pulling behind it what seemed an enormous black sea monster, or the world's biggest sausage; this apparition contained fresh water. When it appeared, men began hurriedly stringing fire hoses up the steep, narrow streets and stairways of Hydra, harried by householders who might have been without water for a few days or a few weeks. Like a great serpent the hose uncoiled itself up the winding paths, came in through the door, and, thrusting its head into the cistern, began to spew water. When it receded again, the householder could pump—by hand, or, if his house was very up-to-date, by motor—the water from his cistern to the tank at the top of the house, and from there it "ran" through whatever plumbing there was. Drinking water, on the other hand, came by donkey from a spring on the island, and was stored in a large Biblical pot in the kitchen. Ice came from the icehouse. Fish and fruit were brought from boats which came to the harbor. Medical attention came from the mayor or from midwives.

We sat aboard the *Toscana* contemplating this beautiful fishing village and barnyard, Hydra, with its flimsy waterfront fringe of Athenian teen-age night life.

A successful Athenian businessman and his wife, who had a summer house on Hydra, came on board for dinner. They were both middle-aged, medium-sized, elegantly dressed, and fluent in English. They were friends of friends, and so we introduced ourselves: Henry McIlhenny, who had chartered the *Toscana* and invited the rest of us on the cruise, Curator of Decorative Arts at the Philadelphia Museum, possessor of a great art collection himself, including some of the pillars of French impressionism; Joseph Pulitzer, Jr., editor and publisher of the St. Louis *Post-Dispatch*, and his wife Louise; the Philadelphia artist and teacher Emlen Etting and his wife Gloria Braggiotti Etting, who was in the midst of her second book and compiling a lecture based on this trip; the young New York composer Charles Turner; Perry Rathbone, director of the Boston Museum of Fine Arts; Mrs. Patricia Clark of Philadelphia, charming widow; and myself, itinerant author.

We asked the couple about the people of Hydra. "Back behind the port live the real Hydriots, who find what work there is in fishing and in construction, and so on. There's not much work for them here. They're very self-respecting. They have their pride, and of course they look down on us Athenians as being weak and corrupted, city people. They have the strong characters of islanders."

"Some of them are superstitious," the wife put in. "Several of the less educated type of men here, after they speak to me, spit! Just like that, matter-of-factly. To ward off the Evil Eye. A woman who works for us here has never been down to the port. She's in her fifties. It wasn't respectable to come here when she was a girl. I'm not sure she's ever seen the sea at close range."

"They get enough money to live," the man went on, "from relatives abroad, as so many Greeks do. You know our families are very tightly knit, and it is the duty of those making money to support the others. Most of the families here have sons or brothers in the Greek Merchant Marine and they send part of their pay back, out of the little they earn. There are only about twenty-five hundred people living here permanently, but this rock won't support even that many."

"To be a Greek man," she said with a twinkle in her eye, "is a very mixed blessing. Dimitris will agree with me here. From the moment they are born they are cherished by their mothers and sisters, they are superior to women, they are served. After they are married they are still free to come and go, they are free, free. Paradise! But how they pay for it! A young Greek man may not marry until his sisters have their dowries and are married. No wonder they serve him! If a Greek man has an ugly sister and doesn't make much money—bachelorhood for life. There are a number here on Hydra."

"But these people here," said Dimitris, "and for that matter all Greeks, have a capacity to enjoy themselves. It's true. That's one thing we really know how to do. We can do it with almost nothing at all if necessary. Have you ever noticed a Greek taking pleasure from a flower, or a cup of coffee? We are able to create a gay party

for twelve people with two pistachio nuts, a half a glass of wine, and a harmonica! We can respond to any encouragement for enjoying life faster than anybody, and go farther with it. We laugh and we make jokes and we sing a lot—we sing to ourselves or together or anywhere—and we like to dance very much. We believe, we *know*, that life is to be enjoyed, and since most people here are poorer than anyone else in Europe or America, you can see how strong this force must be in the Greeks, to be so strong in spite of so much misery, economic misery. We feel it in our bones, life is to be enjoyed. There's an engine always running inside a Greek, something like a generator building up the potential for joy. When you switch into that, out it pours!"

"It helps to be a little crazy," his wife put in. "All Greeks are that, too. There's something called the Greek Madness. We don't have all those complexes you go to psychiatrists for in America. No. Nothing as ambiguous as all those American complexes. But a Greek has one devastating obsession inside him. Scratch a Greek and you will find an obsession."

"I think we haven't completely forgotten our old gods," said Dimitris. "We all still think that if we achieve some one wonderful thing, why we'll go straight to Olympus, to immortality! Either that, or else we sometimes suddenly throw our lives away."

Around us, in the great natural amphitheatre crowded with white houses, the night sounds of Hydra were asserting themselves, the crazy roosters breaking out at any and all times, crowing back and forth across the silent rooftops, donkeys braying agonizingly, and now and then a shriek from the cats.

The Hydra tribe of cats gave the impression that if the human population diminished just a little more, the cats would take over the island. Their scarred, emaciated bodies moved not only stealthily but rapaciously among the tables of the agora. As I learned later

when living on Hydra, one of them in the black of night might drop like an infiltrator onto the window sill, and calmly explore around you as you slept. If you woke up and hissed or yelled at it, the cat would glower steadily back at you for a while and then coldly withdraw—for a while. Or in returning to your house you opened the front door and there was a sudden scrape of claws and a ragged shape, or two, or three, shot by you and out the door. You felt relieved, because they had bolted for the door and not for you.

After dinner on the *Toscana* we started in a group along one side of the port to a foot-road cut into the rocky hillside above the sea; turning into this little road we encountered the moon, clarion clear in the ash-black sky, spreading a wide field of silver on the black water. Big and little stars were scattered everywhere around it, and the lights of other islands on the horizon could be seen past the great shadowy palisades which lined the coast of Hydra like the bastions of a vast fortress. A tiny motor launch with a fringed cloth roof puttered slowly across the sea; on board some people were singing one of the convoluted, dirgelike songs of Greece.

We came to a kind of night club in a one-story stone building where, until recently, small boats had been built. There was one still there, suspended from the ceiling, and another served as a bar. In the dimly lit room the young set, mostly Greek, danced to popular European songs and American rock-'n'-roll and Greek music.

At the bar I suddenly found myself next to one of the young Greeks who had taken part in the rescue that afternoon. He was drunk. "Somebody gave me whiskey and so," he said with a wide and happy grin, "I am drunk." I said that he had a right to celebrate after the rescue that afternoon.

"You know something?" His eyes narrowed, the direct manner became point-blank. "I didn't do it for her. I did it for myself. For the glory. I and all the others went in to save her because we saw a chance for a little bit of glory. I was furious because the others went in and they were all furious too. We all wanted to be noticed, we all wanted a chance to—distinguish ourselves. How are we going to do anything in Greece, make any kind of mark, be *remembered*? Be successful in business? There's hardly any success for anybody in Greece. I will earn four thousand drachmas—a hundred thirty-three dollars a month, and so will my friends. I will live with my wife in a house like theirs, our clothes will be the same. I can't show what *I* am myself, there is no way to show that, except by some extraordinary act. I would gladly die in a war if I could be a hero, I don't care about dying, because then I would have done something and distinguished myself. Well," he shrugged, "I did my best today. I pulled one-sixth of a fat lady out of the water. I guess I'm not immortal yet, though, am I?"

Out the window went my concept that the nobility of classical Greece survived there today, and then it came back in again. What else had inspired the ancient heroes, and even more, the ancient rank and file—at least after heroically repelling the Persians—except glory, unless it was the even less noble goal of money and booty? "Stranger, go tell the Spartans that we lie here obedient to their commands." Don't let them forget us and what we have done. Remind them about us. Us.

Delos was dead, beautiful, and strange. The wind of the Aegean swept over its few acres, slid around its one physical feature, little Mount Cynthus, drifted among the fields of ruined palaces and temples and theatres, and touched no stir of life anywhere.

Coming up to the island by boat was tricky, because of this wind. We approached along a narrow and shifting channel between Delos and the island of Rhenea. Two reefs cut the surface of this channel, and there was a strange sea running, a brilliantly blue and subtly

Hydra

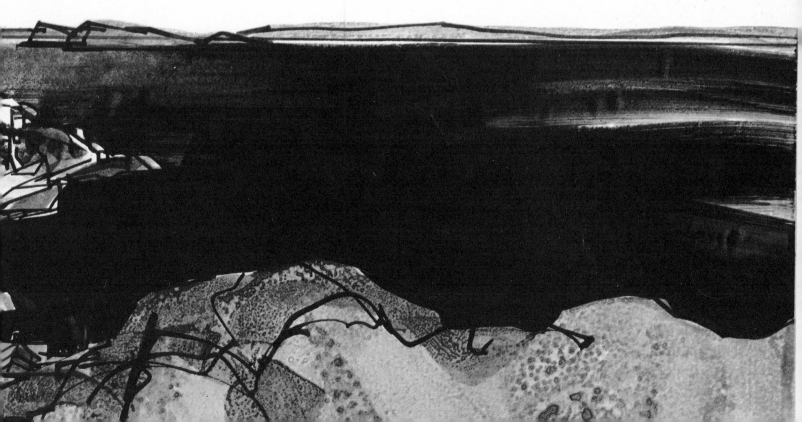

The Cats of Hydra

difficult sea. Little rocky peninsulas of the island reached into the channel, and around them the water was a glowing, luminous green. Across it all the capricious wind of the Aegean swept now in one direction, soon in another, brushing up silver on the surface of the sea and ruffling the weeds of the island. Everywhere there was movement and shifting colors and changing currents and doubt. Only the wrecked monuments of Apollo stood immovable at the center of all the flux; and at the center of the center, there was a broken stump of a once-great statue of him, powerfully carved in white marble, a part of the torso and legs, twenty-five hundred years old.

We disembarked and started into this sanctuary. Delos is three miles long, less than one mile wide. It is greenish-brown now, and there are very few trees. Mount Cynthus, the towering climax of the island, from which Zeus watched the birth of Apollo, is just 368 feet high. Except for the statue of Apollo, which must have been huge, everything about Delos is rather small and careful, on the scale of humans. Taste and harmony dominated what was made here. The central square, the Sacred Way, the Sacred Lake, the amphitheatre, the Temple of Apollo itself, were not awe-inspiring. The awe was apparently supposed to come from Apollo; from his shrines, there only came beauty. Even the Delian lions are about the size of real lions, which they only somewhat resemble. Archaically carved in white marble, seated on their haunches, their long, rib-showing bodies tense, mouths gaping, they have confronted the wind of Delos for twenty-six hundred years and have been wind-changed to the sleekness of sea lions, roaring still through worn-away heads. They face across the Sacred Lake, which is dry now of course—all the Apollonian waters everywhere are dry—and full of rushes and a few palm trees. Behind it there is a little museum, where many very beautiful statues and fragments have been gathered from around the island. Next to the museum there is a small guesthouse, the only other nonruin on Delos.

Few visitors were there this summer day, and no guide was in evidence. Gloria Etting and I ventured along toward Mount Cynthus. She was taking pictures. We passed the smallish amphitheatre,

its central half-circle of stage restored, with a trough circling beneath it where rain water flowing down the bank of stone seats was caught and led into a subterranean cistern. Weeds grew among the semicircle of seats, and soil had flowed down and carried away the upper rows.

She stopped to take some pictures, and I wandered on through the remains of Hellenic houses, rooms opening on a colonnade which surrounded a central, roofless court. Usually there was a mosaic on the floor of the courtyard, perhaps a beautiful dolphin in green, blue, and white, or an elegant black-and-white abstract, a Picasso-like man with a flute, a splendidly stylized trident, a gorgeous panther with Dionysus riding on his back. I threaded on through the narrow, turning way, past the walls of these two-thousand-year-old homes, and at a corner found Gloria again. "I went into that temple," she indicated a classical marble structure the size of an important living room, "to take a picture of that statue, the woman's figure with the beautiful drapery. Who is she?"

"She's the Egyptian goddess Isis."

"And from every direction lizards ran out at me. 'Get the hell out of here' is what they were saying, 'Get the hell out of here with your camera.' I never got the picture."

Staying with each other, we went on to the summit of Mount Cynthus. There was a pedestal, some rubble, nothing else living or dead.

The sea, deeply blue except for the glowing green pool in which Delos floated, stretched far away into the mist, where the faint but formidable outlines of much larger islands hovered on all sides—Andros, Syros, Tenos, Mykonos, Naxos, Paros—forming a circle around the tiny hub of Delos. These were the Cyclades, the Circle, and there was another ring of islands outside these inner seven. The Cyclades occupy the center of the Aegean, halfway from Greece to Asia Minor, and in ancient times their power was considerable and their strategic importance tremendous.

Looking from the horizon down on Delos I could see the ivory-colored temples, the white pillars, the pink walls, the lovely miniature ruins of the ancient Delos of Apollo. Far down another slope there was a small, circular threshing floor, and six horses were being driven around it like the hands of a clock. A little growing was being done here now, but the people who did it lived on Mykonos. Nobody has tried to live on Delos for a very long time.

Delos had everything once. First of all it was the birthplace of Apollo, the god of light, beauty, intellect, art, music, and poetry, who was the link between the world and the other gods, the god the Greeks loved most, embodying their ideal of manhood, the symbol of their spirit of reason and measure, Apollo the Beautiful, Apollo who Spoke. Delos became his sacred sanctuary some time before history began. In the fifth century B.C. all the dead bodies were dug up and moved away, to heighten the island's purity, and no one afterward was allowed to die or be born on Delos. A sudden, unexpected death had to be followed by elaborate purification ceremonies. Pilgrims from all parts of the Hellenic world came to Delos for the great festivals to Apollo with gifts for the god's treasury, with money to build still another temple or another palace; the Delian citizens themselves, rich and cosmopolitan, erected still more theatres and public buildings and shrines and monuments. The festivals increased in ambitious splendor every year, with elaborate competitions in music and dancing and poetry, with horse races and theatre, the Athenian contingent arriving once by a glittering bridge thrown across from the island of Rhenea. Many nationalities established themselves and their gods, and their art, on Delos under the protection of Apollo. At the beginning of the fifth century B.C. the Persians swept through the Cyclades—but kept a respectful distance away from sacred Delos.

As if this spiritual pre-eminence and artistic richness were not enough, tiny Delos began to demonstrate a strong talent for commerce. It had the last good, small but good, harbor before Asia Minor, and since it was impervious to the turmoil of wars or pirates, traders by the thousands made their headquarters there. Immense riches rained down on the little island, and, by the second century B.C., it was one of the greatest commercial centers of the Mediterranean.

And then time began to run out for Delos; it was running out for Greek civilization itself. Time began to overtake even Apollo, who held sway for so long over the minds and destiny of Hellenes. Apollo was a god, but he was not immortal; he lived on belief, and belief was growing weak.

In 88 B.C., during a war between Rome and Mithridates of Pontus, the latter suddenly struck at Delos, so extremely rich, so traditionally defenseless, and after all vaguely allied with the enemy, Rome. It was a sacrilege, but could Apollo really defend himself? Twenty thousand people were slaughtered in a day, and nothing was left standing on the island.

The next year the Romans retook it, for even after such a thoroughgoing sacking Delos retained its good harbor, and perhaps some vestiges of its spiritual authority. The Romans patched it all up as best they could, succeeding to the point where Delos once again began to look tempting. So pirates swept down in 69 B.C., destroying everything, stealing everything, and taking the people as slaves. The Romans lost the defenses they had built on Delos.

But there was no longer anything much to defend. Neighbors began sailing over to carry off some of the marvelous marble for building on their own islands. Athens was by now the "protector" of Delos, but there was nothing of any practical use there any more, just ruined beauty, just history. The island was put up for auction. There were no takers.

The Lions of Delos

TIME IN GREECE

There was nothing "timeless" about Greece. Everything had a rather definite place on the ladder of past time and that was why it seemed accessible to us, why we could imagine something of what it was like, why its reality was still so strong. There had been many changes but no interruption between what Homer described in the *Odyssey*, what Odysseus saw and did on his voyage, and what we were seeing and doing now, two thousand eight hundred years later. It was all connected. The Greek people understood this and took it as an unremarkable matter of course: on Samos they still often talked of Pythagoras, their native son who had made good and done them proud; on Cos the people practically knew Hippocrates personally and thought he was fine although a slight bore by now.

No American is ever placed in time with this kind of Greek certainty. The past of an American trails back a few generations and then must make the leap across an ocean and lose itself in a vague earlier family history in one or two or three or four old countries somewhere. In Greece they knew that they had been there for thousands of years and that everything was likely to go on and on and on.

THE LIGHT

Greece is a stage. The famous clarity of the light there—you can see the contours and depth of a small hill four miles away—makes it a beautifully illuminated stage. That must be why drama was invented there, and why the first masterpieces of the theatre were Greek.

The light had one other quality; it seemed to be right. In many parts of the world the light didn't look right; it seemed to be bleaching the colors, for example, or blurring contours, or making things look garish, and it tended to have correspondingly distorting effect on your feelings, making you vaguely depressed without reason, or a little disturbed or a little shrill. But in Greece the light was right.

BAREFOOT IN KALYMNOS

Harralambos [a friend and guide on Kalymnos] had two sisters, one more beautiful than the other. They were about sixteen and eighteen years old; one was fair with dark wavy hair, a beautiful figure, and a forthright, laughing attitude despite the Greek requirement that as a girl she somewhat efface herself in public. The other was darkish blonde, and looked like a goddess of classical Greece. Both had slightly almond-shaped dark eyes, and self-contained, content expressions. You would have thought two such girls would have been the result of generations of carefully nurtured life with all of the advantages, flowers from the hothouse.

Here was their house, two concrete-floored rooms for four people. It had electricity but no other twentieth-century convenience. The girls were barefoot; both wore the simplest cotton dresses. Their environment was virtually outside what we in the West think of as civilization; it was a world of donkeys, cobbled streets, bare rock, barehanded toil, simple to primitive everywhere. Not, however, in the training of the mind. Harralambos was qualified for and going to attend engineering school in Athens the following year. Both the girls spoke competent English and read a lot and knew a lot.

Barefoot in Kalymnos, they carried in themselves the paradox of all Greece: civilization at the bottom of the economic ladder, flowers in aridity, people marked still by the marvel of the classical Greeks, but barefoot; the vestiges of a past greater than any other all around them, but in ruins; studious and complicated minds, but unemployed; beautiful, but in rags; full of vitality, but trapped in the idleness of no opportunity. That was Greece.

Nothing further has happened to it during the last two thousand years, except for work by archaeologists recently. The Mykonots use it as a sheep run.

And Apollo? In the fourth century A.D. the Roman emperor Julian the Apostate, trying to turn Rome back from its new Christianity to the old gods, sent a famous doctor, Oribasius, to Apollo's other great shrine, Delphi, on the mainland of Greece. From it had come the oracular pronouncements that for centuries had rung through the Greek world. In the depths of a great temple a priestess sitting on a tripod, and aided, it is believed, by a mysterious vapor and a sacred spring and a sacred laurel tree, would go into an ecstatic seizure and babble out the answer to a supplicant's question. The heroes and rulers of Greece had trooped to her; war, life, everything, hung on her poetic, ambiguous pronouncements, for she was the earthly voice of Apollo.

So Julian's doctor went to Delphi and brought back to the Emperor this message, the last heartbroken words ever spoken by the oracle: "Tell the Emperor that the bright citadel has fallen to the ground; Apollo has no longer any shelter, or oracular laurel tree, or a spring that speaks; even the vocal stream has ceased to flow."

The poignancy of wrecked beauty was everywhere, in the courtyard of a weedy palace with the mosaic as bright and alive as ever and all else worn and time-changed beyond imagining; a husband and wife in white marble, her robe draped with the grace of flying water, standing without heads in the devastation of their home; a colonnaded street with all the pillars broken; and most of all the sense still of bustle and prosperity, of full, busy houses all now facelessly ended, done for thousands of years ago. On every side the wreckage evoked their confidence and their accomplishments, the great underground cistern and its row of stone arches holding intact still today, and even water at the bottom, sickly green, with a frog floating on it. During the great contests of music and singing at the festivals of Apollo, Delos had been awash with melodic voices and the vibrance of strings; the silence there now was like an alarming vacuum, like the silence that follows the abrupt cessation of a great orchestra when there is no audience; ruined, the stump of Apollo in white marble was awkwardly propped up, like some terrible relic of a saint's body, grotesquely preserved. Delos was the gutted light of ancient Greece, at the mercy of every passing wind, of any traveler with itchy fingers, of any stray goat.

The wind had been rising steadily all morning, and now it seemed that it was the real *meltemi*, the "bad wind" of the Aegean Sea. As we came aboard, Michelis the sailor said in his fundamental English, grinning widely, "Is blow. Bad. We go Mykonos now. Nice. Music. Big restaurant. We go before wind stop us. No want stay Delos. Delos," a Greek twist of the hand, "finish."

When we left the Cyclades, we sailed back across the Aegean to where the first sight of the mainland of Greece appears. This was Sunion, where the Temple of Neptune still faced the sea from its noble, ultimate headland, and where the sun happened to be setting with fantastic beauty and drama, and where someone said that life in the Aegean islands was certainly very hard but that it was lived, and lived naturally and in its own terms, fully, unlike so many lives in parts of the world where life was easy, and that on the whole and in spite of the incessant hardships of poverty, the islanders had what counted most, a full life lived naturally.

John Knowles has written widely for magazines and is the author of two novels, Morning in Antibes *and* A Separate Peace. *This article will form part of his book* Double Vision: American Thoughts Abroad, *which is to be published in June by The Macmillan Company.*

Delos

DRAWINGS BY ARNO STERNGLASS